LA DOLCE VITA

LIVING IN ITALY

LA DOLCE VITA

LIVING IN ITALY

CATHERINE FAIRWEATHER

PHOTOGRAPHS BY

MARK LUSCOMBE-WHYTE

A BULFINCH PRESS BOOK
LITTLE, BROWN AND COMPANY
BOSTON NEW YORK LONDON

First United States Edition

ISBN 0-8212-2751-3
Library of Congress Control Number 2001090607

First published in Great Britain in 2001 by Pavilion Books Limited

Designed by David Fordham

Bulfinch Press is an imprint and trademark of Little, Brown and Company (Inc.)

Set in Serlio and Fournier
Typeset by MATS, Southend-on-Sea, Essex
Colour reproduction in England by Anglia Graphics
Printed and bound in Italy by Conti Tipocolor, Florence

Quote on page 21 from *Casa Guidi Windows*, Part One (1848) by Elizabeth Barrett Browing.

Picture credits for prelims: page 1 shows the tiled dining room in the Palazzo Belmonte; page 2 shows the staterooms of the Palazzo Lanza Tomasi; page 3 shows an archway within Castello Depressa; page 5 (from the top) shows Torre di Bellosguardo, Calcata and Giammetti's apartment in Rome.

Picture credits for chapter openers: pages 10–11 (clockwise from top left) show the terrace at Castello di Villadeati; the side entrance at Castello Depressa; a view of Villadeati; an archway at Palazzo Belmonte; Sandro Chia's vertical garden; Castello Ruspoli; a fresh lemon on a tree; windows with shutters; a view of Castello del Romitorio; wine from Feltrinelli's estate; a patterned floor at Belmonte; and the suspended gardens at Castello Ruspoli.

Pages 92–93 (clockwise from top left) show the view from the "dovecote" in Avane; Casa Pagani; an alcove in Il Monastero; Gaia Servadio's terrace; detail of a plant; peacocks at Avane; fresh fruit in a bowl; a view of Avane; a detail at Il Monastero; and the worn steps at Avane.

Pages 152–153 (clockwise from top left) show Pellini's conservatory; Giammetti's library; Alistair McAlpine's hat collection; a detail from Pellini's apartment; McAlpine's dog; Giammetti's upper terrace; Venetian glass at the McAlpine apartment; Pellini's *fin de siècle* nostalgia; classical busts at the McAlpine apartment; a lily; Pellini's crystal and glass; and Giammetti's apartment.

CONTENTS

INTRODUCTION

ABOVE *The decorative effect of thick, stuccoed walls, rough beams and terracotta flooring is at once rustic and elegant in its simplicity.*

LEFT *A converted roadside chapel constitutes the theatrical sitting room of Amedeo Pagani's summer retreat in Puglia.*

I TALY'S REPUTATION FOR GOOD LIVING is hard to play down. Who has not been seduced by the myth of *la dolce vita*: the easy-going Mediterranean lifestyle – a spontaneous hospitality combining lingering lunches with friends and family, and the flow of wine and conversation? Who has not harboured a fantasy of taking off to live in this fabled country where culture and history are as integral a part of the fabric of life as good food, hospitality and sunshine?

Some of the artists, writers, designers and collectors featured in this book have done precisely that, rising to the challenge of resurrecting homes, often from crumbling ruins and piles of stone, in an ancient and beautiful landscape. But then, as the great Italian modernist Gio Ponti once quipped, Italy is a country created half by God and half by architects, and here Mark Luscombe-Whyte's photographs give us a taste of both. The book takes us through the interiors of inspiring private universes – cottages and castles, farmhouses and urban palazzi in glorious "God-given" surroundings, from the foothills of the Alps in the north, through the lyrical landscapes of Tuscany, the hidden hunchbacked lands of central Italy and down to the plains of Puglia and the rugged volcanic islands off the coast of Sicily.

The Irish writer Molly Keane once described the typical English country house as sitting low and comfortably in its valley, as cosy as a teacup in a saucer. Italy, on the other hand, is remarkable for its castles and country houses, which invariably perch atop hillsides like splendid tiaras and crowns. Take Inge Feltrinelli's exuberant baroque folly, which soars over the fertile vineyards and orchards of Piedmont, or Gore Vidal's imperial villa wedged vertiginously in a clifftop on the Amalfi coast. Then there is photographer Stefano Massimo's extraordinary troglodyte home, which seems to grow out of the rock that supports it in an unknown corner of northern Lazio. We also visit the forbidding battlements of painter Sandro Chia's Tuscan monastery and Lady Lennox-Boyd's fortified castle in the Sabine hills, both looming over the horizons in landscapes that are

7

anything but gentle or comfortable. Such lofty architecture will, however, always guarantee, at the very least, a "room with a view".

Italian houses often hide away their splendour behind high anonymous walls; the writer Gaia Servadio's cottage in Stromboli or film producer Amedeo Pagani's retreat in Puglia are cases in point. And in this book we gain privileged access to the inner sanctums of these homes, stepping behind the walls that normally hide these exotic houses from the outside world. The fashion designer Romeo Gigli opens up his apartment in Milan, the artists Maro Gorky and Matthew Spender welcome us into their splendidly bohemian farmhouse in Chianti, and we visit the grand interiors of palazzi that might have sprung from a film by Visconti, including the real-life version in the ancestral Palermo home of Prince Giuseppe Tomasi di Lampedusa, author of *The Leopard*, the novel that depicted so evocatively the lifestyle of the declining aristocracy in Sicily.

These are interiors that inspire with their sensual response to beauty, illustrating that very Italian instinct for architectural and decorative harmony, and balance of colour and design. Twenty very different homes celebrate the past as much as they embrace modernity. But above all these are interiors that are bought to life by the personalities, the idiosyncratic tastes and temperaments of a group of fascinating and talented individuals, natives and foreigners, artists and aristocrats, who inhabit them. It is a book as much about the people who live in the homes as about the decorative environments they have created for themselves.

ABOVE LEFT *A collection of eighteenth-century seals and hunting horns makes a sophisticated display on a mantelpiece in Piero Castellini's Tuscan retreat.*

ABOVE RIGHT *Romilly McAlpine's changing room and original Anthony Little bed beyond.*

RIGHT *Rustic minimalism is the style found in the hallway and stairwell of the Guinness's house.*

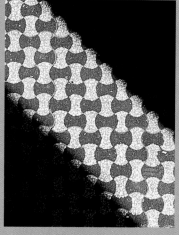

GRAND STYLE
CLASSIC VILLAS AND COUNTRY ESTATES

THROUGH THE CENTURIES Italy has been the most invaded land in Europe, and noblemen protected themselves by erecting fortified edifices on high ground. The concept of the villa as a courtly country building was a phenomenon of the development of architecture during the Renaissance, not just an expression of defence but as a symbol of status and artistic merit. From the terraces of a flamboyant Baroque pleasure-dome in Piedmont on Italy's northern frontier to the hidden interiors of a country estate in the deep south, this chapter features the ancestral homes of the ruling elite. These are enclosed, private universes. While plumbing and electricity have bought these grand estates into the twenty-first century, we open the door on undiminished interiors that retain a sense of elegance and grandeur, where tradition and the spirit of the past, both historical and personal, are ever palpable.

CASTELLO DI VILLADEATI
PIEDMONT

INGE FELTRINELLI

ABOVE *An arch-framed view of the flamboyant eighteenth-century façade.*

LEFT *Villadeati, for all its apparent exuberance, is about compositional elegance of architecture, with special attention given to the proportions of different structural elements.*

BELOW *Inge Feltrinelli, on the upper covered gallery.*

PIEDMONT, THE MOST NORTHERN REGION of Italy, rises from the flat plains around the River Po in an undulating succession of grassy hills, before meeting the girdle of ice and rock that make up the Apennines and the Alps.

Villadeati is some fifty kilometres east of the regional capital Turin, tucked away in a green and fertile valley of orchards, rice and wheat fields. This is not only the bread basket of Italy; it is a gourmet's larder rich with white truffles, wild mushrooms and the heady Barolo and Barbaresco wines. The gentle patchwork landscape of vine, meadow and pasture is punctuated by mulberry, elm, willow and neat rows of poplar, which are as emblematic of the region as the cypress is to the Roman Campagna or the umbrella pine to the south.

Vulnerable through history to invasions by the Byzantines, then the Goths, Lombards and Franks from the north, it is an area characterized by hilltop castles and fortified hamlets. The feudal overlords attempted to control their domains from incursions by foreign invaders and local dynastic rivals by building battlements at strategic vantage points. The Castello di Villadeati stands on high ground that was ancient contested territory between the dukes of Savoy and the marquises of Monferrato. However, by the time the land was acquired by one Giacinto Magrelli in the late 1700s, the need for a fortified castle had become redundant. The patrician ideal was the country villa reinvented as a gracious retreat and surrounded by formal geometric gardens with airy loggias and panoramic belvederes. In an area rich with magnificent *castelli*, the "pleasure-dome" that is Villadeati is perhaps the most surprising and bewitching of all.

Villadeati was bought on a romantic whim in the 1950s by Inge and Giangiacomo Feltrinelli when this corner of Italy was considered embarrassingly unfashionable. It was a total ruin, and the couple camped in their car during visits to monitor the progress of the extensive

RIGHT *A view down to the terracotta rooftops of the village below, over the multi-tiered garden terraces with airy loggias and panoramic belvederes. Secret underground steps lead to the village, and the turret pictured would originally have served as a lookout post. Feltrinelli imported a variety of exotic plants including palms and limes from Cuba, which flourish in the temperate climate.*

FAR RIGHT *The gardens and terraces of Villadeati are a kind of theatre to surprise the senses. Built in the Baroque style, this ornamental garden comes complete with fountains and romantic arbours, grottoes and statuary. The statue pictured here is found below one of the terraces leading from the orangery.*

renovations. Now widowed, Inge Feltrinelli, the venerable and irrepressible head of Italy's most dynamic publishing house, uses Villadeati to entertain friends, writers and publishers, and as a weekend retreat from Milan.

Intriguingly, she refers to the place as her cottage folly. It seems the most unlikely of descriptions when you first spy Villadeati from a distance, rising above the humble roofs of the village like some glittering multi-tiered confectioner's fantasy. Only when you step inside the house do you realize that the sweeping external proportions of the palace are deeply misleading. This butterscotch-yellow creation of colonnades, turrets and balustraded parapets cascading across steeply terraced gardens is purely decorative, built for show. The main living quarters, two storeys high and one corridor wide, are indeed cottage-like in their intimate dimensions. The entire edifice is simply an extended, exuberant, architectural flourish.

While the identity of the architect and the exact date of the building remain a mystery, Villadeati is thought to have been constructed in the late eighteenth century in the school of Juvarra, the pre-eminent architect of the period. He created the Italian equivalent of Versailles at Stupinigi, and was celebrated for his flamboyant lines and his sense of theatre. Magrelli, a lawyer and evidently a prosperous and aspirational member of the new professional class, set about commissioning a daring residence that would not only embrace the pervading baroque architectural fashion but would celebrate his wealth and display his refined sensibilities to the world. A pleasure-dome, then, to inspire a sense of leisure and relaxation. Thus the two colonnaded wings spread from the central axis and tower like a pair of open arms in welcome, linking the landscape to the house.

The garden, you sense, was created not so much as a haven of peace and quiet but more as a stage set for gentrified social rituals – a kind of theatre, a place of discovery and entertainment. Finding your way around the falling levels of terraces, joined by spectacular ramps, tunnels, frescoed galleries and flights of steps, is indeed a sort of adventure. The design of the garden constantly plays tricks with the light and the sense of perspective. Shadowed archways are broken by sudden shafts of sun to vary the architectural rhythm. Each walkway gives onto yet another lookout point to exploit the far-reaching views and shifting dimensions of the façade. Here are the grottoes, fountains, niches and statuary so beloved of the Baroque: landscape gardening conceived to jolt, surprise and refresh the senses.

While the outlying terraces of the garden are planted with vines and vegetables, Feltrinelli has also imported a variety of exotic plants from abroad, which flourish in the temperate

16

ABOVE *The Christmas baubles decorating the mounted stag's head in the library are a visual joke in keeping with the playful spirit of the house and its exuberant architecture.*

LEFT *The internal spaces of Villadeati, so extravagant and grand on the outside, are deceptively small and modest. A narrow spiral staircase runs the height of the central tower to circular rooms that have no function other than to provide dramatic vantage points from which to enjoy the all-embracing views. Next to the staircase in the cloakroom alcove is a poster promoting Prince Lampedusa and his seminal work* The Leopard, *published by Feltrinelli.*

climate. Lime trees from Cuba, now nearly four metres high, tower beside rosemary hedging studded with banana trees and date palms. There is a covered avenue of vines alternating pink, purple and white grapes that particularly delights Feltrinelli.

Built originally for fun and pleasure, Villadeati is still a wonderful location for parties. "I will quite happily invite 500 people for cocktails on the lawns beyond the orangery. But the great thing is that it is also a house that is conducive to solitude. I come here to be alone. Escaping to my bed with a pile of manuscripts is my idea of pure relaxation." And this being a house of a woman who has made a life and a career out of her passion for reading, it is appropriate that books are everywhere. They furnish the interiors, wedged high like a contemporary art installation against a wall in the drawing room and piled across every surface of her bedroom. They cram the floor-to-ceiling shelves of the study and fill the corners of the bathrooms and cloakrooms beneath framed promotional posters of authors that testify to an eventful career and a history of extraordinary friendships. (It was Feltrinelli who discovered both Lampedusa and Pasternak and made *The Leopard* and *Dr Zhivago* two of the greatest literary successes of the twentieth century).

Only the elegant circular room in the central tower matches the exterior in its grandiosity. This is a graceful frescoed and columned space, which Inge Feltrinelli has deliberately left free of clutter, allowing the triumphant view over the cascading terraced gardens to speak for itself. Unpretentious comfort, however, is the main keynote of these interiors, which borrows something of the cheerful and cosy, or *gemütlich*, style of the owner's native Germany. Cheerful and colourful ornaments clutter the surfaces, and shiny Christmas baubles hang like earrings off the antlers of a mounted stag's head as a sort of visual joke. Sofas and armchairs, upholstered in her favourite shades of orange, acid green and red, all betray an exuberant personality that is well in keeping with the abiding vibrant spirit of the house and its exhilarating blend of brio, playfulness and fantasy.

TORRE DI BELLOSGUARDO
FLORENCE

AMERIGO FRANCHETTI

THE ENGLISH WRITER JULIAN BARNES once observed that when we dream of France we are really dreaming of Burgundy. In the same vein, perhaps our dream of Italy is simply a dream of Tuscany. Certainly, not even assiduous film-makers like Merchant-Ivory could have invented a view more eloquent or closer to our fantasy of Italy than the one from the rooms and terraces of the Torre di Bellosguardo. It is a landscape of nature improved by the art of man. Between hazy silhouettes of cypress and hill, the terracotta rooftops of Florence, punctuated by Brunelleschi's dome, Giotto's Campanile and the tower of Palazzo Vecchio, shimmer below.

THIS PAGE AND OPPOSITE
Threatened by attack from rival clans, medieval residences around Florence were built with lookout towers (right). This fourteenth-century tower is part of a sixteenth-century building, with its upper loggia (below) embracing views over Florence and its enclosed garden (left) with original terracotta floor.

> *From Tuscan Bellosguardo*
> *Where Galileo stood at night to take*
> *The vision of the stars, we found it hard*
> *Gazing upon the earth and heaven, to make*
> *A choice of beauty.*

As Elizabeth Barrett Browning describes, this is the spot where Galileo is said to have come to read the stars, a place that so enraptured Dante and his friend Guido Cavalcanti that the latter decided to build his home here. It became known as the Torre di Bellosguardo.

Today, Bellosguardo is a quiet leafy neighbourhood of grand villas and gardens just a ten-minute drive from the centre of Florence. The road narrows between high ivy-cloaked walls and zigzags around the hillside before drawing up at an elegant avenue of cypresses that leads to the Torre. The square thirteenth-century tower from which the villa gets its name would have served as a lookout post against unfriendly strangers in the late Middle Ages. The villa itself is a sixteenth-century addition, a fine Renaissance façade frescoed with the now fading

21

graffiti of the heraldry of former proprietors – six emblematic hills to represent the family's property and wealth. A marble statue of Charity by Flemish artist Francavilla hovers above the arched lintels of the entrance. Such architectural embellishments were popular features in the suburban villas of the newly rich banker and merchant class of sixteenth-century Florence. It was a subtle advertisement for the cultural refinement and the social distinction of the inhabitants within.

The Medici and, later, the Michelozzi families who lived at Bellosguardo set about improving the original fortified structure of the tower, converting its battlements into a patrician residence. A loggia laid with an intricate pattern of terracotta floor tiles was built and an internal courtyard with an adjacent warm and light-filled *limonaia* added. The artists of the Renaissance had recently discovered the art of perspective and liked to play tricks with the space. Hence, the frescoed panels of stylized birds and fruit in the dining room, and friezes depicting scenes from the Old and New Testament around the walls of the ballroom, exploit the sense of perspective and artistically inflate the proportions of the room.

Baron Franchetti inherited the property from his grandmother, Marion Hornstein, after the Second World War. In the 1920s she liked to take in paying guests, and the visitors' book is filled with the names of eminent figures from the Arts and members of the European royalty.

ABOVE LEFT *A centuries-old avenue of wisteria separates the landscaped part of the eighteen acres of property from the vineyards, orchards and vegetable gardens.*

ABOVE RIGHT *The lofty spaces, soaring vaulted ceilings and classical proportions of the rooms are softened with decorative techniques popularized during the Renaissance. Stylized floral designs frescoed onto window architraves are reminiscent of Roman wall paintings.*

RIGHT *A grand staircase carved out of the local* pietra serena *stone leads up from the entrance hall to the* piano nobile.

After her death and a decade that saw the villa reincarnated as a finishing school for American students, Amerigo Franchetti decided to resuscitate the traditions inaugurated by his grandmother. Intensive restoration works lasting eight years ensued, and the Torre finally reopened in 1988 as an exclusive and discrete hotel. The Baron and his wife live in a smaller adjacent lodge in the park but continue to use the elegant spaces of the Torre for entertaining, piano recitals and festivals.

All sixteen bedrooms have been refurbished with antiques and the sturdy mahogany furniture characteristic of the Tuscan style. The elaborate coffered and painted ceilings were restored and the panelling repaired. So lofty and grand are the natural proportions of the rooms, it is easy to feel dwarfed even under the spreading brocade canopy of a sumptuous four-poster bed.

The eighteen acres of terraced park and garden are equally atmospheric. Franchetti, who was educated in England, which included a period at Cambridge, has introduced English ideas about plants and gardening into the classical Italianate design scheme of the park. Neat sculpted parterres and walls of box hedging are planted over with climbing roses, honeysuckle and plumbago, combining an Italian formality with the more artless abandonment of the English style. Similarly, formal water and rose gardens are broken up by romantic pergolas and arbours beneath the shade of magnolia and blowzy wisteria trees that are hundreds of years old. Within this scented and enchanting oasis, all is *"luxe, calme et volupte"*, to quote Charles Baudelaire, and the outside world is very much kept at arms' length. As one particularly enraptured guest wrote in the visitors' book, "This is a place to come to refresh the spirit and remember that life is good."

ABOVE *The banqueting room, with its decorative ceiling, contains the coat of arms of the previous owners, the Michelozzi family, above the fireplace.*

ABOVE LEFT AND FAR LEFT
The main salon with its impressive frescoed and vaulted ceiling by artist Bernardo Poccetti, dates from 1580. The two faux doors on the back wall lead nowhere but help create a sense of symmetry and balance.

LEFT *Elements of the building's fortress origins remain in the heavily bossed wooden doors opening onto one of the private suites on the ground floor. This is the oldest part of the building. Before being turned into a gracious villa, the tower stood isolated, and these massive doors would have protected the inner sanctum from intruders.*

RIGHT *Despite the spare, functional simplicity of the furniture and furnishings, these interiors are architecturally extravagant. Theirs is a grand style which is all about the intrinsic beauty of a fine floor, a carved panel, a painted wall and a supporting arch or column. These are structural and decorative details that enhance the luxurious feeling of space. The now much-faded fresco above the bed depicts a bucolic scene of picnics and revelry and dates to the beginning of the twentieth century. The Victorian gothic panelling, or* boiserie, *is antique pine, copied from an estate in northern Italy.*

CASTELLO DEL ROMITORIO
TUSCANY

SANDRO CHIA

ABOVE *The imposing structure of Il Romitorio looms over the vineyards.*

LEFT *In the dining room, there is an eclectic mix of objects – a flying angel found at a local market, a painted tableau on cloth, an English art deco sofa and ornate copper chairs from India.*

BELOW *Sandro Chia and daughter, pictured through a window.*

THE WALLED MEDIEVAL CITY OF Montalcino in Tuscany is where Leonardo da Vinci is said to have painted his bird's-eye view of the world. It sits perched on a lofty hill above the Via Cassia, the ancient road connecting Siena to Rome, once the well-trodden way of penitents and pilgrims. It is on this magnificent but tough and exacting land, in the shadow of Montalcino, that the imposing silhouette of the Castello del Romitorio looms. A former monastery, built on a remote and rocky outcrop, it was always seen as a place of sanctuary by the hermit monks, a place conducive to a life of meditation and contemplation.

Despite the austerity of their existence, the monks always loved their wine, and from the Middle Ages this chalky, unyielding soil was found to be good for the vine. Today, the fat sangiovese grape produces the famous Brunello di Montalcino red which, matured for no less than four years in oak barrels, is a wine of extraordinary rich, full-bodied depth.

Sandro Chia is a painter and sculptor who became celebrated in Italy and America for bringing back a sense of painterliness to art. Now the proprietor of this former hermitage, he produces 35,000 bottles of Brunello wine each year on the surrounding seventy-five acres of land. At the foot of the fortress he has built an enormous cantina for their storage. Its façade features a vertical garden with shrubs of the classic Mediterranean *macchia* interspersed with Sandro's marble and bronze sculptures and the odd strategically placed architectural fragment. As a wine grower, he obviously relishes the physical and spiritual connection to the soil. He likes to say the ancient practice of cultivating the grape is "an art form in itself". Like the painter who makes considered choices about each pigment he uses, the wine grower selects each grape deliberately.

Recently Chia decided to dedicate himself full-time to this land. Gone are the houses in New York and London, and the Castello del Romitorio, this bastion of austerity, has become the

LEFT AND ABOVE LEFT
Il Romitorio makes no concession to decorative frivolity. A bare landing and staircase make an effective backdrop for the strong, bold lines and spirit of some of Chia's own work. On the landing stands an early Chia etching and at the foot of the stairs is a table featuring three bronze sculptures.

ABOVE AND RIGHT *The poignant symbolism of the angel, which dominated the imagery of the high Middle Ages, recurs in Chia's work. A bronze angel (above) decorates a side table, while (right) two tall, single-winged angels hold a heart in the entrance hall, with its rare original stone floor and Roman trough. Between the wrought iron crests is Chia's design for the label of the first wine produced on the estate.*

LEFT *A strong decorative effect is achieved in the study by grouping together different pictures. Chia found a stack of empty frames in the house, cleaned them and filled them with his own work. He has given a spontaneous and irreverent twist to the anonymous 1930s portrait of a woman by sticking a red plastic star to the glass front. Indian cushions are from Camilla Guinness's shop in Buonconvento.*

ABOVE *A Chia sculpture and photograph frame, a gift to his wife.*

ABOVE RIGHT *The view from the dining room, showing an eighteenth-century Italian chair and Indian scrittoire, leading into the study where an ancient sarcophagus is displayed above the bookcase. These interiors are intentionally left under-furnished so as not to detract from the integral austerity of the architecture.*

permanent base for himself, his sons from a previous marriage, his wife, the writer Marella Caracciolo, and their growing family.

For Sandro, the first sight of the Romitorio was an instant *coup de foudre*. There was something about the rigorous symmetry of the edifice, with its fortified towers making no concession at all to decorative frivolity, something about the silence and impenetrability of the thick stone walls, that spoke volumes to him – despite the roofless, dilapidated state of the building, choked by ivy and colonized by wandering sheep and swallows.

His friend Giorgio Franchetti had bought the place, but had not moved in – his young wife found it too forbidding and stark, and even locals refused to linger long after dark. But by the end of an autumnal afternoon in 1984, Sandro had convinced Franchetti to sell. Since then he has installed electricity and bathrooms to make the place habitable and has repaired the gaping holes in the roof. He has built a bell-tower for the adjacent chapel, in which his little daughters were baptised and which has also served on occasion as a convenient lean-to for his collection of vintage and modern motorbikes. He has taken bulldozers to the land and removed stones "the size of

ABOVE AND ABOVE RIGHT
The recurring image of angels forms part of both the internal and external decorative scheme. This statue in the garden, of an angel holding a bronze heart, is by Chia.

RIGHT *Chia's skylit studio with its 1930s leather armchair, art deco lamp and cabinet displaying what Chia refers to as his "pirate's treasures", includes Etruscan amphoras and Indian silver pillboxes. Chia's own paintings and sculptures live in perfect harmony with works by other artists.*

igloos", as Marella puts it. And on the surrounding plains, once the feudal battlefields of warring Florentine and Sienese armies, he has planted row upon row of neat vines facing south.

There is an overriding sense here that the castle has a soul that cannot so easily be tamed, despite efforts to soften the fortress-home with books and comfortable English furniture piled high with cushions. Not even the attempts to create cosy dens for children, building fairy-tale bunk beds in their nursery, or any amount of central heating and electricity can hold back the spirit of the past. "It is still haunted with the ghosts of ancient knights, still inhabited by all forms of wildlife, crickets, lizards and birds who find refuge amongst the nooks and crannies of the battlements", Marella explains.

And the spirit of the past, both religious and pagan, medieval and mythological, evidently continues to haunt Sandro, whose figures of centurions and angels appear over and again on his canvases, which he now executes in a separate studio. There is a Bacchus for the design of the labels for his wine bottles and a Madonna on the flag design he created for the Palio Siena's famous horse race. Sandro's paintings are bold and huge. He is similarly a man of solid and formidable physical stature. With a brow as impenetrable as the Romitorio itself, you get the sense he needs and relishes the space of this medieval monastery and its lands, both for the sake of his canvases and for his own physical and emotional well-being.

34

CASTELLO RUSPOLI
LAZIO

CLAUDIA RUSPOLI

ABOVE *Claudia Ruspoli pictured with her favourite dogs.*

ABOVE RIGHT *Boxwood hedges in the Renaissance suspended garden.*

LEFT *The sixteenth-century fortified entrance, carved from local peperino stone, is surrounded by a moat with a drawbridge. The coat of arms over the portal reveals an unmistakable mark of ownership; it commemorates the union in 1530 of two dynasties.*

THE HAUNTING EXPANSES OF NORTHERN Lazio – a honeycomb of temples, tombs and caves and hidden passageways carved into the soft, porous tufa rock – is the heartland of an enigmatic culture that pre-dates the Romans. This is land of "the long-nosed, sensitive-footed, subtly-smiling Etruscans / Who made so little noise outside the cypress groves..." (DH Lawrence, *Cypresses*). And towering over the ruins of just such an Etruscan settlement is the imposing grey stone and crenellated edifice of Castello Ruspoli.

The palace's fortified corner bastions and moat dominate the landscape of the little town of Vignanello, about an hour's drive north of Rome. A drawbridge brings you to the portals of the castle – stern, forbidding and crowned by the family coat of arms. There is no doorbell here; instead, an outsized iron claw serves as a knocker. A chorus of savage barking from within is accompanied by a sound of heels across a stone floor. Donna Claudia, the latest in a long line of energetic and dynamic Ruspoli princesses who have resided here for four centuries, pulls open the door, a modern-day chatelaine dressed in jeans with an enormous bunch of keys hung around her neck. With her sister, she inherited the palace several years ago. "I used to come here as a child during the summer months," she relates, "and it was something of a penance for me. With these massive stone walls and the great gates I felt like the damsel incarcerated in the tower."

Now the place consumes all her energies. Her first priority was to restore and open the grounds to the public – these are some of the best-preserved Renaissance gardens in Italy. Claudia's formidable forebear, Ottavia Orsini, originally planned them in the sixteenth century when the ground was raised over the valley and connected to the castle by means of a drawbridge. The space was divided up with formal boxwood hedges of laurel, cherry-bay and

37

ABOVE *The well, in which the family saint Giacinta fell as a child and emerged miraculously unharmed, and the carved fifteenth-century font where she was baptised. Born Clarice Marescotti in the castle in 1585, Giacinta was canonized in 1807.*

LEFT *The stone plaque, once mounted by the roadside, commemorates Francesco Maria, who ruled the estate from 1705 to 1731. Stone relics from the ruins of the previous church decorate this alcove off the major staircase.*

RIGHT *The hall, with its wide herringbone floor and vaulted ceiling, is ideal for summer dinners. Wrought-iron gates open onto the armoury where, centuries earlier, the night watchman was posted.*

ABOVE *One of the grand salons, decorated in hand-painted* papier peint, *depicts the heraldic hills of the Ruspoli family. This salon is also the scene of the murder of Sforza Marescotti by his wife Ortensia.*

RIGHT *Lit by candles and warmed by the fire from a vast hearth, the main dining room reveals oil paintings of ancestors from the 1700s beneath an original wooden coffered ceiling.*

myrtle. These and the sixty-four lemon trees in terracotta urns placed at the corners of each compartment are still in place today. Ottavia's initials and those of her two sons, Sforza and Galeazzo, also remain sculpted into the hedges centuries after they were originally created. Meanwhile, Santino, who has been with the family for thirty years, is busy clipping and pruning, employing the same techniques of cultivation and maintenance that have been handed down over the generations.

Below the parapet is the so-called "secret garden" with neat parterres of tulips and iris. These border the Etruscan caves that used to house the olive presses, which Claudia dreams of one day converting into an underground swimming pool with mosaics. Beyond these formal enclosures, nature reigns free. The once elegant avenues are wild and overgrown to the point where the undergrowth has almost disguised the medieval pillar of justice at the old gates. Here the

LEFT *Above the doorway of the smaller stateroom hangs an eighteenth-century portrait of Francesco Maria Ruspoli with his adored dog. A monochromatic frieze from this period, bearing the crests of Ruspoli and his wife, runs above the brocade-covered walls. The rich brocade was a popular way to furnish a room, providing a warm and lustrous expanse of textured colour.*

RIGHT *When Pope Benedict XIII visited Castello Ruspoli in 1725 to consecrate the church, he left behind his tunic, slippers and hat as a gift.*

BELOW *A detail of an ancient manuscript, or printed book, which is displayed in the small stateroom.*

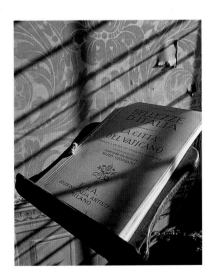

condemned were once manacled to the column and whipped. The stone has been worn smooth by the pinned-back elbows of the unfortunate victims. It serves as a grim reminder of a past beset by the bloody rivalry and conflicts among the various local seigneurs struggling for ascendancy.

The estate of Vignanello was passed from one noble family to the next until 1531, when Pope Paul III bequeathed it to his niece Ortensia, upon her marriage to Sforza Marescotti. He was the founder of the Ruspoli dynasty, and with the help of the renowned architect of the period, Antonio da Sangallo the Younger, they turned the medieval fortress with its warren of narrow passageways into a majestic palace. But the course of family history, even then, did not always run smoothly, and Ortensia murdered her husband in one of the salons. She eradicated all signs of him from her life and defaced his coat of arms above the fireplace, which, to this day, displays its vandalized marble heraldry to the world.

ABOVE *Ceilings often form part of the overall design scheme in Italian palazzi. Here, celebratory frescoes of the Virtues were painted on the bedroom ceilings in honour of the papal visit of 1725.*

RIGHT *Intricate Italian craftsmanship is visible in the altar, which has been painted to resemble marble. Private places of worship were habitual parts of the architecture of the grandest Italian palaces. When Giacinta was made a saint in 1807, a chapel on the ground floor was built in her honour.*

FAR RIGHT *At Castello Ruspoli, grandeur does not always preclude comfort. The opulence of this bedroom comes from the ancient hand-printed linen from the early 1700s, fabricated in Caserta in southern Italy. Floor cushions from India and a kilim turn the bedroom into a cosy retreat.*

The staterooms make little concession to the twentieth century; only the family's private apartments are heated. Much of the decoration is as it was when it was painted in honour of a papal visit in 1725 – still unquestionably grand, if a little faded. Lively frescoes of the Virtues adorn the bedroom ceilings, although the brocaded wallpaper is worn and peeling at the corners. A monochromatic *grisaille* frieze from this period depicts hills and grapes, the heraldry of the Ruspoli dynasty, in the salon where Sforza Marescotti was dispatched and still crowns the *papier peint* wallpaper.

Considering its gruesome history and despite its stern appearance, Castello Ruspoli is a remarkable place in which to live. When Claudia fills the state rooms of the *piano nobile* with mimosa, positions Roman flares along the battlements and lights the fires in the giant hearths, when the one hundred candles in the chandeliers are lit and the terracotta floors are buffed to a deep gleam, when the drawing room throngs with the guests who come to listen to a recital of Handel (once a frequent visitor to this home), it is easy, then, to imagine the sound of hooves clattering outside the battlements and feel the twentieth century slowly melting away.

PALAZZO
PARISI

LAZIO

ARABELLA LENNOX-BOYD

ENTRAL ITALY, WHICH CONTAINS THE ancient land of the Sabines, is a hidden hunchbacked land of darkly-forested hills capped by walled and shuttered villages. These are not so much sleepy as semi-deserted, apart from the odd stray cat or old woman wearing her loneliness in black. A region ravished by the invading Roman army in 390 BC, it has been wracked by poverty for centuries. Today's inhabitants have mostly decamped to Rome which, although only an hour's drive to the south-west, could be in a different country altogether.

Tourists hardly ever venture up these twisting roads to the forgotten village of Oliveto, where the celebrated garden designer, Lady Lennox-Boyd, born Arabella Parisi, spent her childhood. Her father Piero Parisi, armed with money to invest, had bought the *borgo* or walled hamlet, with church, chapel and a sixteenth-century fortified villa, sight unseen, during the First World War. Arabella's mother, Irene – a famous Roman beauty – fell in love with the place and made it her retreat, quite literally, from the world and society. "The house was so much part of her," says Arabella, "that when she died, I didn't know if I could bear to return." But, for a couple of weeks each year, return she does. The family can no longer claim territorial rights over the entire village, but the chapel and the broad, bare, unembellished structure of the fortified house remain theirs.

It has become a lot more comfortable than she remembers from her childhood. "In those days, just getting here was an adventure. It would take a day's trip by donkey from the Via Salaria, with a ritual picnic lunch at the old mill. There was no electricity and no running water. We would collect water from the village pump. I learnt to walk upright by balancing the jug on my head. But as the *fonte* provided the only opportunity for chatting to boys, it was a duty we enjoyed."

ABOVE LEFT *The covered loggia off the* piano nobile *has far-reaching views over the surrounding medieval towns and woodland.*

ABOVE *The owners attempt to scare off pigeons with a cut-out cat.*

LEFT *Lord Lennox-Boyd's telescope, set up at the dining room window.*

ABOVE AND RIGHT *Original early nineteenth-century frescoes restored by Arabella's daughter, the artist Dominique la Cloche, add depth and interest to the dining and drawing rooms, extenuating the space with their idealized landscapes between* trompe l'oeil *marmarino columns painted to resemble pink marble. Italian style often prizes art above nature, thus a panel or column that looks like marble is more desirable than the real thing.*

Back then, it was a working farm – a *fattoria* – and the villa retains this air of bucolic charm. The "peasant palazzo" is what her English husband Mark likes to call the place. Arabella's mother bred ducks and chickens, incubating the chicks in her bedroom. She became so attached to them that they never made it to the stock-pot but took over the mattress instead. They must have been the only chickens in history to have been granted the privilege of roosting beneath the silken canopy of a bed that once belonged to Napoleon's sister. Its ornate Florentine-Empire design still dominates the space in their bedroom. Another wall is taken up with mementoes of her grandfather, the great Italian war hero Armando Diaz, who defeated the Austro-Hungarian army at Vittorio Veneto. Here is the painting presented to him by Native Americans on a victory tour of the United States. His drawing pencils are still in the original 1920s' cartons stamped with his title and crest *Duca della Vittoria*, Duke of Victory.

ABOVE *A terracotta plate displayed on a wall.*

LEFT *From the Renaissance onwards, decoration was lavished on walls and ceilings, as shown in the billiard room here where, in the 1500s, the Principe di Santa Croce came to deliver law and justice. A frescoe depicting his coat of arms and triumphant banners adorn the wall above the vast travertino marble fireplace, which is closed off in the summer with elaborately painted doors. The billiard table also dates back to the 1500s, while the mounted antelope's head is a hunting trophy from a trip made to Kenya by Arabella.*

ABOVE *The owner furnished the house largely, in her own words, on a shoestring from odd pieces of furniture, such as the bathroom sink which she found languishing in an attic.*

RIGHT *The lace and brocade curtains pictured in Arabella's father's bedroom and in the bathroom were accrued over the years from flea markets in Italy and abroad.*

ABOVE *Detail of a simple bedside Madonna and rosary.*

ABOVE RIGHT AND RIGHT *In the master bedroom, a marvellous silk canopied and gilded Florentine-Empire bed, which once belonged to Napoleon's sister, dominates the space. It makes a strong decorative statement, which is toned down by keeping the other furnishings in the room low-key. A kilim livens up the carpeted floor.*

Arabella's decorative style, however, borrows as much from her adoptive English home as it does from Italy. There is an old Colefax & Fowler wallpaper in the bathrooms where bottles of Floris sit next to tubs large enough to drown in. The main drawing room is furnished with oversized chintz sofas, windows dressed with ruched saffron-coloured blinds and round tables with "skirts" – this is vintage English country house style This marriage of aesthetics and lived-in comfort is the hallmark of the Villa Parisi interior. "The proportions of the rooms may be grand," says their owner, "but really there is nothing of value. It is all pulled together on a shoestring with bits and pieces I found lurking under dust sheets in the attics and cellars." However, the original and elegant stucco detail of the walls, the terracotta urns and tiled floor, waxed deep red (to keep the dust away), and the scenes of a gentrified landscape of castles framed by pines and cypresses on the nineteenth-century murals, remind you that this is patrician Italy.

The cheerful flotsam and paraphernalia of family life and the varying obsessions of its members encroach on all the living spaces of this house. A fax machine in Arabella's office hums beneath a constant stream of paper, although she says she tries to avoid work when she comes to Oliveto. Here, she even refuses herself a garden. With clients including The Duke and Duchess of Westminster, Lord Palumbo, Conrad Black and the Queen of Belgium, and with awards for Best Garden at the Chelsea Flower Show, the renowned garden designer complains that at Oliveto she manages only to kill off her olives and her orchards. She has, however, landscaped the grounds around a spectacular swimming pool at the end of the garden, which is suspended over the battlements with far-reaching views across the valleys.

You sense that this is a woman with irrepressible energy whose enthusiasm is hard to contain. Numerous straw hats and gardening shoes abound in the hallway. And even the grandest room in the house has been taken over by her and her husband's hobby-horses. Elaborately frescoed, with courtly *stemmi*, or coats-of-arms, this is where Vatican officials would come to administer provincial law. An imposing oil painting of the Principe di Santa Croce hangs over the scene. He used to reside in the house in the early 1500s and would terrify the villagers by exploiting his *droit de seigneur*, his sleeping rights over the local maidens.

The former courtroom, now decorated with antlers and hunting trophies brought back from Arabella's trips to Kenya, has become the billiard room, where the sixteenth-century table lies buried under mountains of history books, encyclopaedias and objects waiting to be repaired by Mark Lennox-Boyd. Mark also happens to be a sundial expert and, like his wife's grandfather, a passionate reader of the stars. He treasures the telescope inherited from an ancestor, set up at the dining room window and trained on Jupiter and Mars. It is a gesture and an object that the Lennox-Boyds must relish, conveying a sense of continuity between the generations and the emotional and aesthetic links between past and present.

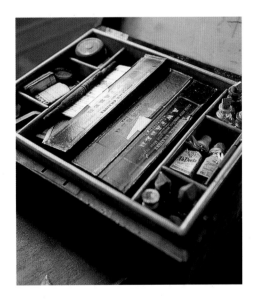

ABOVE *The 1920s drawing pencils and pencil case belonged to Arabella's grandfather, the Italian war hero Armando Diaz, who carried them with him on his campaigns. They are stamped* Duca della Victoria, *Duke of Victory.*

LEFT, ABOVE AND ABOVE RIGHT *These views from the study show the entrance hall with all the paraphernalia of daily life, and the master bedroom and guest wing. The Roman terracotta floor tiles throughout the palazzo have been restored and gain their lustrous glow and depth from a coating of red wax, which is applied three or four times a year to keep dust away.*

LA RONDINAIA
AMALFI COAST

GORE VIDAL

"THE ONLY DELECTABLE PART OF ITALY", wrote Boccacio in *The Decameron*, "is the coast of Malfie, full of towns, gardens, springs and wealthy men." That was in the fourteenth century, but the writer was neither the first nor the last to be smitten by the beauty of the Sorrento peninsula and the Amalfi Coast. First discovered by the emperors and elite of ancient Rome, who built their summer villas here, this verdant but craggy land of lemon blossom and olive, of emerald sea and kaleidoscopic light, has long been a source of inspiration to artists and writers.

King Ferdinand I helped make the region more accessible to travellers with his white-knuckle drive from Sorrento to Vietri. The death-defying stretch of road blasted from the cliff-face was completed in 1852 – fifty kilometres of dazzling sea- and mountain-scapes punctuated by hairpin bends, blind corners and dank tunnels. The road winds through the little towns that cling to the cliff and twists wildly around the precipices and ravines that plummet into the Tyrrhenian sea far below. From Amalfi – once a powerful and independent medieval maritime republic – the road corkscrews up through the Lattari mountains to Ravello. Veiled from the coast by early morning mists, it perches three hundred and fifty metres up on a rocky promontory; "an earthly heaven... of blue sky and sea, gray limestone and olive", as Vidal has described it, according to Fred Kaplan's biography.

No traffic penetrates the narrow streets and alleys bordering the Arabo-Norman pastel-tinted palaces. Mounted ceramic plaques above the entrances boast of former famous residents who found sanctuary or inspiration here; from Richard Wagner to Virginia Woolf, from Greta Garbo to André Gide, and, most recently, Gore Vidal .

The four hundred-metre distance from the cathedral square to the villa of the maestro (as Vidal is referred to locally) is accessible only on foot. Obeying directions "to continue straight, turning neither left nor right until you can go no further", the approach takes you to the outer boundaries of the town,

into the ten-acre estate through a series of gates. Beyond an inviting indigo-coloured swimming pool, a cypress-lined path nudging the ridge of the cliff leads to the evocatively named villa itself, La Rondinaia, or Swallows' Nest. Backing onto the rock face, it seems to teeter on the very edge of a sheer precipice overlooking a melting horizon of blue. It is a magnificent eyrie with celestial views, and the sense of splendid isolation is broken only briefly by the sound of a pleasure cruiser chugging far below. The amplified voice of its guide can be heard urging the tourists to crane their necks skyward where "portside, ladies and gentleman, at the summit of the cliff is the residence of the famous American writer and honorary citizen of Ravello, Gore Vidal". When this famous citizen emerges in person at the doorway, he looks suitably distinguished and quite unfazed by his status as a major tourist attraction.

With arched doorways and windows and tiled floors from neighbouring Vietri, the villa, built on several levels into the lip of the cliff, is a brilliant feat of architecture and engineering. Light, airy and perfectly proportioned spaces, with high vaulted ceilings, fireplaces and symmetrically presented windows, have been calculated to create a sense of equilibrium and balance. This

ABOVE AND RIGHT *The* salotto *is furnished in a grand and opulent style with an eclectic collection of oriental lacquer tables and objets d'art, sixteenth-century tapestries, eighteenth-century paintings and heroic statuary from ancient mythology, including this first-century dragon mosaic mounted as a wall piece. Other favourite possessions are a second-century Graeco-Roman bust of Zeus, which migrated with Vidal from New York to his apartment in Rome before meeting its final resting place at Ravello.*

LEFT *These are light, extravagantly proportioned rooms where the artful layout of architectural features such as fireplaces, windows and doors creates a sense of harmony and equilibrium. The grand decorative style suggests an almost classical sense of order and balance, with attention paid to the formal and symmetrical arrangement of furniture and pictures. Here, matching sofas frame the coffee table in a guest suite.*

architectural harmony makes La Rondinaia one of architect Richard Rogers' favourite houses. Built in the Norman-Saracenic style, the villa is actually only seventy-five years old and, even more surprisingly, is not the work of a professional architect.

Originally the land formed part of the estate of the Villa Cimbrone owned by Lord Grimthorpe, an Englishman who designed London's Big Ben. On Ravello's highest spur of land, jutting out over the sea, he created an extraordinary garden embellished with pergolas and neo-classical temples, loggias and grottoes. There is also the famous belvedere, which, lined with the marble busts of classical heroes, embraces a view that seems to stretch to infinity. Vidal, visiting this spot in 1940 by jeep from Amalfi with his friend Tennessee Williams, marvelled at so much beauty. He must have little suspected that, thirty years on, he would be living in imperial splendour himself on a ledge just below this terrace. But that all came later. In 1915 Lord Grimthorpe bequeathed a triangular, ten-acre plot of land to his daughter Lucy, and she commissioned the building of La Rondinaia not from an architect but a local tailor, Nicola Mansi, who had helped design her father's Moorish palace

LEFT AND RIGHT *Seventeenth-century canvases line the hallway (left), which leads off from the main entrance hall with elaborate wrought-iron grilles (right), past Vidal's study.*

BELOW *The indigo swimming pool is set amid cypress pines in the centre of the ten-acre garden where Vidal cultivates lemons, fruit and capers.*

fantasy. It did not remain a family home for long, as during the First World War it was requisitioned by the Allies and turned into a hospital. It's not hard to imagine what those convalescing British officers would have made of the place – it must have seemed an unearthly paradise.

It was Howard Austen, Gore Vidal's companion of forty years, who discovered the villa was for sale in the classified section of a Roman newspaper. Although it needed work, it was an unbelievable bargain and in 1972 it was theirs – the perfect summer retreat, which only later became a permanent residence. The previous owners, Vidal explains, found its inaccessibility too much for their ageing limbs. He, too, as his biographer recounts, moved in staggering, not from any sense of physical frailty but beneath the weight of his most treasured possession, a second-century Roman bust after Antinous, which he insisted on carrying himself all the way from the central piazza to the front door. It had travelled with Vidal for the better part of half a century from New York to Rome and now to Ravello which, he proclaimed, would be its, as well as his own, final resting place.

Today, the bust sits in the grand salon surrounded by other heroic statues from ancient mythology, including a priceless Roman mosaic floor mounted on wall brackets. Inlaid tables, ornate gilded mirrors, tapestries, eighteenth-century paintings and oriental ceramics and lacquerware contribute to the grandeur and opulence of these interiors. Light floods in through graceful arched glass doors that lead on to innumerable wrought-iron balconies and terraces that are a feature of the villa. These framed views are frankly distracting. Is it possible to become immune to such beauty? Gore Vidal sweeps the question away: "It doesn't matter where you live," he insists. "It is just a house. I live inside my head."

RIGHT *Gore Vidal writes on an old Smith Corona typewriter in a study furnished with shelves displaying collections of every book he has written. Magazine and first-edition covers have been mounted on the study door. The motto* Vague Monsters Lurk Beneath the Surface *sits as a framed reminder on his desk.*

PALAZZO BELMONTE
CAMPANIA

ANGELO BELMONTE

LIKE THE SOLID GOLD AND SAPPHIRE crest of the medallion around his neck, sometimes the past weighs heavily on the shoulders of the last Prince Belmonte. With twelve titles, over one thousand acres of mountain and coastal terrain in southern Italy, including this sprawling palazzo, to his name, upholding the fortunes of a dynasty can be something of a burden. And it is a dynasty that stretches back to the invading Longobards of the eleventh century, and includes four cardinals, a pope and a clutch of politicians and ambassadors, one of whom, Antonio Pignatelli, signed the peace treaty between Napoleon and the Kingdom of the Two Sicilies.

But it was another ancestor, Parise I, who, two centuries earlier in 1600, built the Palazzo on the Cilento peninsula, one hundred miles south of Naples. Standing in a protected landscaped park with acres of space and elegant staterooms, it was actually a hunting lodge, never a permanent residence for the Belmonte family, whose main base remained in Naples. But during the shooting season, the Kings of Spain and Italy would descend to the Cilento to take pot shots at the quail and the wild boar that still roam the surrounding forested coastal estates.

Today, it is the only remaining part of an inheritance that once included vast swathes of land and palaces in northern Spain and Puglia. Like the eighteenth-century Sicilian Prince Salinas in *The Leopard*, Prince Lampedusa's famous book detailing the fortunes of a declining aristocracy, Belmonte certainly does not know all the rooms of his rambling palazzo by heart. He might, like Salinas, believe that this is the only kind of house worth living in. But, somehow, the three acres of pitched terracotta tile have to be maintained, and Belmonte has had to be inventive in order to prevent the whole edifice from crumbling around him. One way was to turn the two wings that were once storage rooms for the annual harvest into a hotel of

ABOVE *Entrance to the courtyard.*

ABOVE LEFT *A view of the palazzo on the edge of the local fishing village.*

LEFT *The intricate majolica floor and the bronze busts of ancestors.*

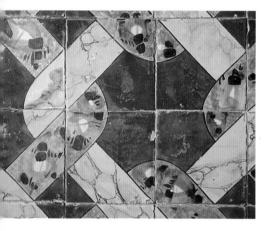

TOP *This copper chandelier is a replica of a Roman oil lamp.*

MIDDLE AND ABOVE *Details of nineteenth-century ceramic ware (middle), and floor tiles in the banqueting room (above).*

ABOVE *Ceramic ware is a striking feature in Neapolitan décor, being cool underfoot yet reflecting sunlight. The clarity of the pigments of these Capodimonte tiles with a high-gloss glaze made from molten glass makes the floor seem modern, yet it dates from the 1800s.*

RIGHT *The banqueting room was designed to ennoble the patron with monumental furniture including a copper chandelier, a vast fireplace bearing the family crest and a gilded ceiling. The doors are a decorative trick, conferring a feeling of continuing space.*

twenty suites. There are still metal loops and hooks hanging from these high vaulted ceilings where every autumn sheaths of corn, figs and carobs were left to dry.

The palazzo, situated on the edge of the little fishing village of Santa Maria di Castellabate, is built in the traditional southern Italian fashion around a central courtyard with cascading bougainvillaea and tumbling plumbago and jasmine. This comes into its own at night when the ancient honeycombed stone, held together here and there with metal girders, is highlighted by the flickering glow of scores of Roman candles. The two remaining private wings surrounding the courtyard house the prince's apartments, which were restored in the early 1980s. Now separated from his English wife, he alone inhabits the echoing corridors where marble busts of his ancestors, displaying the same proud aquiline features as his own, stand sentinel.

His life is a busy one, visiting his estates, activating plans to extend the "hotel" and build another swimming pool, and to develop the nature reserve of Punta Licosa. The peninsula is his passion. Named after the mythical siren Leucosia, the daughter of Cadmus and Harmony, who is said to have saved Ulysses's life, this part of the Tyrrhenian Sea is nothing if not awash

PALAZZO
BELMONTE

ABOVE *Intimacy meets grandeur here, where despite the twenty-foot ceilings and the floor-to-ceiling bookcases groaning under the weight of family documents, the library is still very much a personal room. The prince's desk is decorated with books and recent family photographs.*

LEFT *The highly glazed ceramic floor, which is original seventeenth century, lightens the sombre effect of mahogany. The glass chandelier is from Murano in Venice.*

with legends of antiquity. It is a favourite place for bathing and picnics, a place where he is invariably found before breakfast, taking his "morning constitutional". "The smell of the Aleppo pines and the peace and sound of the sea set me up for the rest of the day," he maintains.

An Italian palazzo without a library or a music room would be an anomaly, and at Palazzo Belmonte these are the two most lived-in rooms, with family photographs, busts, maps and ancestral trees narrating the recent as well as the distant history of the dynasty. In the library, with its floor-to-ceiling mahogany bookcases, the most impressive feature is the shelves of leather-bound copies of every edition of the major southern Italian newspapers right up to the time of Garibaldi. There are also rare, embossed versions of the classics in French, English and Latin.

Doors open onto a series of other less-used rooms, including the chapel with a portable altar in walnut wood. It enabled the extended family, especially the female contingent, to pray privately without stepping foot off the estate, and was a way of ensuring that the patron of the house, Belmonte's grandfather, could control even the divine aspects of everyday life both at home and at large.

Although Angelo, the last Prince di Belmonte, leads a life in several respects quite unlike that of his forebears, when he entertains, it is always in similar old-fashioned style. Alfresco dinners take place on the suspended gardens of the belvedere, which overlook the landscaped gardens and the sea, or, more sedately, in the staterooms of his palace in the winter.

FAR LEFT *Mahogany bookcases cover every inch of wall space in the library, which contains a rare collection of histories, leather-bound copies of newspapers from the 1800s and precious family documents – all accumulated by the present prince's great-great-grandfather who was Minister for Culture. A marble fireplace is carved with the Belmonte crest and family motto.*

The furnishings within the main banqueting room are in the neoclassical style; the heraldic shield and emblem, the nineteenth-century bronze statuary, antique maps and crested Neapolitan plates on the walls are designed to accentuate the grandeur and glories of a family's courtly past. They are the classic decorative hallmarks of a patrician residence. French windows open onto balustraded balconies overlooking the Bay of Salerno and dummy doors that lead nowhere embellish adjacent walls; both aggrandize the dimensions of the room and confer a luxurious feeling of continuing space. The luminous, geometrical design of the blue and yellow floor tiles from Capodimonte reflect the rays of the sun and help to extend the perspective.

More intimate dinners tend to take place in a no less formidable, separate panelled dining room, furnished with swords and armoury given as gifts to the prince's ancestors and with mounted antlers of endangered species on the walls. At the end of a dinner he rings a silver bell to summon the coffee and his wandering minstrels for his favourite form of relaxation, singing along to the melancholic Neapolitan love songs. On such occasions Palazzo Belmonte is the breathing embodiment of a lifestyle taken from the pages of *The Leopard* – "the sense of tradition and the perennial expressed in stone and water – of time congealed".

ABOVE *The crested* baldacchino, *or canopy, was used during the election of the Pope in the Sistine chapel and belonged to a late uncle, a cardinal.*

LEFT *The entrance to the private chapel reveals wooden pediments crowned with a cross above the mask of the devil, symbolizing the coexistence of good and evil. The oil painting is of Pope Pius X.*

RIGHT *The private chapel where estate workers would come for prayers.*

CASTELLO DEPRESSA

PUGLIA

RICHARD AND ELIZABETH WINSPEARE

ABOVE *Olive oil and wine are still cultivated on the Depressa estate.*

ABOVE RIGHT *The nucleus of the estate is the main enclosed courtyard concealed behind heavy protective gates and a high stone wall.*

LEFT *A grand staircase, carved from the soft local* pietra leccese *stone and crowned with the Winspeare coat of arms, leads from the courtyard to the principal living quarters and* piano nobile.

PUGLIA LIES IN THE EXTREME SOUTH-east of the Italian peninsula, caught between two seas, the Ionian and the Adriatic, across which you can see Albania on a clear day. Strategically positioned on the cusp of western Europe and the Orient, the region is a crucible of history, a melting pot of different cultures and customs inherited from the successive waves of invaders who claimed these shores as their own – Greeks, Romans, Normans, Arabs, Turks. To appreciate the region "is to leap across time to the Middle Ages and antiquity", as art historian Paul Homberton suggests in *South Italy: A Travellers' Guide*. "You have to set out to visit Magna Grecia and the glittering cities of Sybaris and Tras; to Roman Apulia, where Hannibal won Cannae, where Horace was born and Virgil died." This quintessentially Mediterranean region is where Hellenic and Latin cultures meet.

One of the many legacies of the ancient Greeks was the habit of cultivating the olive, a tree that had previously existed only in the wild. And today, pushing south into the dry flat lands of the Salentine Peninsula at the very tip of the "heel", you pass acre upon acre of these rocky olive groves encased by low stone walls. The vast, gnarled and twisted trunks of trees thousands of years old make the olives trees of Tuscany seem stunted and puny in comparison. Olives became and remain the wealth of Puglia. The sixteenth-century oil barons who grew rich on these exports in turn secured their work force and their wealth by enclosing their estates within fortified walls. These *masserie fortificate*, the fortified farmhouses that are a striking architectural feature of Puglia, are agricultural complexes consisting of externally plain square enclosures built around a central courtyard. The self-sufficient microcosms usually embraced a noble residence, some homes for the workers, a chapel, some barns and various other useful outbuildings.

Depressa, the seat of the Winspeare family, is one such home. Tucked away behind a high sandstone wall at the edge of a sleepy village of the same name, its foundations date back to the fourteenth century. Continuing the agricultural traditions of old, the family cultivates the olive, as well as the dry and brilliant Salentino wine that goes so well with the intense flavours of the produce from this region. The oil and wine are either exported or sold in son Francesco's shop in the neighbouring town of Tricase.

Baron Riccardo "Dickie" Winspeare's origins and name are not in fact Pugliese but English. Three hundred years ago, a Winspeare orphan was shipped off from Yorkshire to Naples to be brought up by a rich uncle. The orphan eventually produced heirs, one of whose descendants married a Pugliese princess. The estate of Depressa was part of her dowry. When the present Baron inherited it in the 1930s, the building had been used as a tobacco drying plant. Rack upon

ABOVE LEFT AND RIGHT *The canine members of the family, Oliva and Albanese, are pictured by heavily bossed main gates (right) which close off an exotic garden of palm, jasmine, pomegranate and bougainvillaea from the street (left shows the side entrance). Traditionally the farm estates, or* masserie, *of Puglia were small fortified castles consisting of plain square architectural complexes built around a central enclosure.*

ABOVE *A stone oil vat has been planted with herbs.*

ABOVE RIGHT *The Graeco-Roman column is the symbolic pillar of justice from the medieval law courts of an ancestral palazzo belonging to the Prince of Tricase. Along the wall in the background is* une allée de mémoire – *a display of memorial plaques for favourite deceased dogs set into the brickwork.*

rack of the pungent crop hung from the rafters of rooms that have since been knocked into one elegant twenty-two-metre vaulted summer salon.

The Baron's wife, Elizabeth, Princess of Liechtenstein, for all her northern genes and cosmopolitan upbringing and education, says she took immediately to the deep south of Italy. The semi-feudal rhythm of life in Puglia was not so dissimilar from the community she grew up in in Hungary. She promptly fell in love with the palace with a less than hopeful name; the name Depressa has its roots in the terrible siege of the area by the Turks in 1480. The local capital, Otranto, was brutally sacked and the incursion wiped out populations of neighbouring villages and traumatized the region. The small community of Salete changed its name to Depressa and so it remains to this day. A relic of this bloody period of history is the large stone cannonballs in the central courtyard, which were launched by the invading Turks.

History is part of the oxygen you breathe at Depressa. Everywhere you look, photographs, coats of arms, plaster seals, oil paintings, books, busts and other objects and heirlooms evoke ancient origins, privileges and family ties. The memorabilia and mementoes accrued over the years, not always of great value, are personal remembrances of times past. It is this, rather than any grand decorative scheme, that defines the peculiarly nostalgic character and languorous atmosphere of the home.

Architecturally, the house borrows certain elements of the southern baroque style, which flourished in the region between the late sixteenth and eighteenth centuries and found its apogee in the exuberant façades of the palaces and churches of the nearby city of Lecce. Depressa is similarly built in *pietra leccese*, the local honey-coloured sandstone perfectly suited to the decorative flamboyance of the time. The stone "that cuts like butter and hardens like

ABOVE *The cabinet is a Neapolitan money chest from the seventeenth century, with panels of painted glass.*

LEFT *Objects and heirlooms that evoke ancient origins, privileges and family ties define the peculiarly nostalgic character of these interiors. Here, the bronze of an ancestor, Antonio Winspeare, graces an alcove above a display of medals and mementoes which recall the Baron's maternal American forebears.*

RIGHT *The twenty-two metre salotto on the ground floor has been recreated out of three separate storehouses once used for drying tobacco. The framed map is over one hundred years old and was bought because it is one of the few maps of Italy that actually pinpointed the small village of Depressa. The porcelain figure of a women on a plinth is a copy of an original by Donatello; the lacquered white furniture is from Venice.*

steel" (HV Morton, A *Traveller in Southern Italy*) could be easily carved into the popular scrolls and curlicues, garlands and friezes that architecturally celebrated the confidence and new-found prosperity of the province.

The central courtyard at Depressa, while not as ornate as some of palaces of the period, nevertheless boasts grandiose and lavish ornamental effects: elaborate porticoes, carved balconies and a crenellated design in bas-relief beneath the parapets. The enclosed space, protected from prying eyes by towering metal-bossed doors, is scented with jasmine and festooned with bougainvillaea and the fruit of the pomegranate tree. Once within the fortifications, it seems a world away from the dusty sun-baked street outside, at once timeless and enchanted. There is a graceful rhythm in the arrangement of arched and mullioned windows around two wings and in the balustraded trail of stairs leading up to a crested doorway. These are the portals that lead into the inner sanctum of the *piano nobile* where the Winspeares live and entertain. A series of salons, bedrooms, study and libraries open off a long gallery, which serves as an orangery in the winter.

But the Baroness's favourite space is the terrace, or loggia, built in the purest Italian style and shaded from the perpendicular southern sun by a lofty vaulted ceiling, with windows offering views over the green of the exotic estate. Palm trees jostle for space next to olives, citrus and a bamboo-garden maze – an extraordinary artifice and a remarkable feature of Depressa. The lush ornamentation of this towering tropical grass is the last thing one would expect to see in this driest region of Italy.

ABOVE LEFT *The heavy, bossed iron door opens onto the inner sanctum of the* piano nobile, *which displays a marble bust of Antonio Winspeare.*

ABOVE *The present Baron put his neoclassical beauty (a copy from the National Museum of Naples) behind bars because he found the idea of an imprisoned soul appealing.*

LEFT *Ceramic tiles from the 1930s surround the old marble washbasin and original wood-burning ovens in the castle kitchens.*

RIGHT *The patron saints, Cosma and Damiano, stand in an alcove.*

PALAZZO LANZA TOMASI

SICILY

GIOACCHINO LANZA TOMASI

THE OLD PALAZZO LAMPEDUSA IN PALERMO, which inspired elegiac descriptions about the declining fortunes and lifestyle of the Sicilian aristocracy in the famous twentieth-century novel, *The Leopard*, is now just a hole in the ground. When the Allies dropped the series of bombs in 1943 that devastated not only the ancestral home but much of the city as well, it is said writer Prince Giuseppe Tomasi di Lampedusa fell into a dazed silence that lasted for days. But a decade later, having salvaged his extraordinary library from the rubble, he moved to Via Butera, the *casa di mare* mentioned briefly in the novel – a rambling palazzo on the seafront where he lived out the rest of his days.

Lampedusa's adoptive heir, Gioacchino, now resides with his wife and child in the same palazzo on the Via Butera, now called Palazzo Lanza Tomasi. Over the last thirty years, he has painstakingly restored it to its former nineteenth-century grandeur by buying back the fragmented sections and apartments that over the decades had been sold off as workshops, stables, a sardine cannery and a shipbroker's office. One wing had fallen into ruin, severely damaged by the same bombs of 1943.

Situated in the south-east corner of the city, this neighbourhood, known as La Kalsa from the Arab word "pure", is the original Saracen citadel that expanded around the harbour in the ninth and tenth centuries. It became the most desirable part of town to live in, and Goethe, the German Romantic poet, thrilled in 1768 at his first view of its "shore with bays, headlands and promontories (that) stretched far away to the left. In front of the dark buildings, graceful trees of a tender green, their tops illuminated from behind swayed like vegetal glow-worms. A faint haze tinted all the shadows blue" (*Italian Journeys*). The poet went on to reside in a house a few doors down from the Palazzo Lanza Tomasi.

LEFT *A rare sixteenth-century coral and silver holy water font.*

FAR LEFT *The nineteenth-century ballroom, with partquet floor, contains Louis XV furniture, consoles and mirror saved from the original ancestral home in Palermo.*

BELOW *Prince Gioacchino Lanza Tomasi and his wife.*

LEFT AND BELOW *An elegant salon off the main ballroom is furnished with pieces inherited by Prince Lanza Tomasi from his mother's palace, including nineteenth-century library lamps in muslin and bronze. The peacock wall colour was discovered under layers of old wallpaper and refreshed. The floors are the original red and white marble. The decoupage screens are French, made with a collage of cut-outs from French fashion magazines of the period. There is a Spanish two-dimensional statue of St Theresa next to the fireplace, continuing the flavour of Spanish Baroque.*

RIGHT *A ceramic Virgin Mary sits between two canvases depicting scenes from the life of St Francis and is by a local painter.*

Today, a marine highway cuts off the shore from the palace, and the celebrated elegance of the district is faded and worn. Despite this, the "tender green" treetops described by Goethe continue to frame the view. Palm fronds still dress the palazzo's eighteenth-century classical façade with its broad, high terraces and the graceful rhythm of the louvred windows beneath alternating arched and triangular pediments. From these, it is an unchanged broad panorama of the same "metallic sea" described in *The Leopard*.

A modest entrance on the later nineteenth-century street façade of the palace leads you off the pavements into an enclosed courtyard. In Palermo, where privacy is sacrosanct and where every man's home is his fortress, the stern and forbidding or simply anonymous aspect of the portals of the nobility tend not to convey a sense of embrace and welcome. Instead, the entrances and doorways give a self-protective impression of introversion, of shutting out the world. Here, only a rare staircase of red Verona marble leading up to the

ABOVE *A nineteenth-century bronze clock, in the romantic style, was recovered from the writer Giuseppe Tomasi di Lampedusa's home.*

RIGHT *Mahogany bookcases house fifty thousand leather-bound volumes in French, Italian and English. Beautifully maintained and arresting original flooring, such as this one in varnished nutmeg and maplewood, enhances the elegance of the spacious, classically proportioned state rooms.*

ABOVE *A marble urn and English trinkets are displayed in front of a 1930s oil painting that depicts the prince's mother.*

inner sanctum of the *piano nobile* advertises the promised splendour and status of the residence within.

This is where, today, Prince Lanza Tomasi, a musicologist and university lecturer, and his interpreter wife, Nicoletta, hold relaxed soirées. "The palace was acquired as compensation from King Ferdinand II when he confiscated Lampedusa island from the family," explains Tomasi. "It was originally used only for entertaining, for celebrations and firework displays during the Santa Rosalina festivities." And so the tradition of entertaining continues in the gracious interconnecting salons. The most impressive feature of these rooms remains without doubt the original library of Lampedusa, containing some 50,000 bound books in French, Italian and English, which Tomasi is slowly putting in order. They are still housed in the original mahogany bookcases salvaged from the Palazzo Lampedusa along with some fine furniture, including Louis XV consoles, tapestries, mirrors and

LEFT AND ABOVE *In the garden Sicilian tiled benches depicting a stylized view of the seafront were retrieved from the original Lampedusa home (above). The statue (left) was part of a vast fountain and represents a standing leopard, which formed part of the heraldry of the Lampedusa family and gave the famous novel its name.*

RIGHT *Looking from the library into the entrance hall, a sixteenth-century Baltic amber mirror sits over the fireplace. It was much prized by the Sicilian aristocracy of the period. The console table with ornate griffins as its base has an unusual inlaid Roman lava stone top. The vases are Russian Empire, and the inlaid mother-of-pearl cabinet in the corner is Sicilian, made by Carthusian monks.*

mantelpieces. The blonde nutmeg and cherry chevron-patterned parquet and cream walls serve as a neutral backdrop for the ornate splendour of the objects and furniture, all of which relate a story; here are mementoes of travel and matrimony, of patronage and inherited wealth. The smallest salon painted in the popular peacock-blue of the neoclassical period is the most ornate and decorative room of the palazzo and a favourite room for retiring with coffee after grand dinners.

The Lanza Tomasis' actual living quarters, though, are below the *piano nobile*, leading off an exotic terraced garden filled with rare cacti and palms. Decked out with the fountains, statuary and old Sicilian tiled benches rescued from the Palazzo Lampedusa, this is a space that evokes all the languor and lazy sensuality of the *fin de siècle*.

Prince Lampedusa wrote of Sicily as a country overburdened with a past for which it has little respect. He lamented the demise of the nobility whose significance, he believed, lay entirely in its traditions and its vital memories. He need not have worried – his adopted heir, living out a life of modest splendour in the old palazzo in Via Butera, has ensured that the fabric of the past, preserved within the walls, the furnishings and objects of the ancestral home, does not dissolve into rubble and dust.

BOHEMIAN CHIC
RURAL AND ISLAND RETREATS

INVARIABLY POSITIONED in hauntingly beautiful and remote corners of the land, these farmhouses, cottages and crofts have attracted a diverse and cosmopolitan group of artists and designers who have converted the once humble peasant dwellings into simple but sophisticated studios, family homes and holiday retreats. In Tuscany, the farmhouses have evolved from primitive farms dating back to the Middle Ages and Roman times. Open-plan living spaces have been adapted from lower floors that once provided shelter for livestock. In the south, rural buildings were influenced by Saracen and Arabic architecture, with small windows facing inwards, thick walls as protection against the heat and internal courtyards conducive to an out-of-doors lifestyle. These are houses in harmony with their surroundings, interiors that embrace natural materials such as terracotta, limestone and thatch, using age-old decorative techniques that reflect the simplicity and purity of the architecture itself.

AVANE
TUSCANY

MATTHEW SPENDER AND MARO GORKY

THE SCENIC CHIANTIGIANA ROAD LEADS you through the green heart of the rolling Tuscan countryside between Florence and Siena. Few landscapes seem more timeless and familiar to the traveller, the earnest eighteenth-century Grand Tourist weaned on the aesthetics of the Italian Renaissance and the camera-toting pilgrim of today. Through undulating hillsides of holm oak, chestnut and pine, the road winds past the ancient Chianti "vineyards of stencilled viridian", to quote Spender, capped in the distance by the loggias and crenellated turrets of the nobility's castles. It was here, to an estate of thirty-two acres called Avane – the place where no wheat grows – that sculptor-writer Matthew Spender and his wife, artist Maro Gorky, came to live in the late 1960s. They moved "on a whim", as Matthew writes in his memoirs, *Within Tuscany*, "to escape the thin blue light of London town". And once their daughters were born they stayed because, Maro quips, "babies cry so much better in Italian".

It is a landscape that has been improved by the hand of man; no better inspiration then for an artistic couple determined to pursue a life of bohemian creativity. Matthew recreates the curves of the surrounding bosomy hills in his garden workshop with sculptures hewn out of local clay or carved from the surrounding woods. These are peaceful and characteristically fecund-looking figures that stand sentinel around the house and grounds. Maro, the daughter of Armenian Expressionist Ashile Gorky, also aesthetically harnesses the natural world around her in canvases that seem to combine qualities of both energy and stillness.

Framed by a long drive of tall cypresses, Avane is a typical Tuscan farmhouse, or *casa colonica*, with the traditional square dovecote-tower and loggia intact. The owners have hardly changed the original structure of the building. According to the date chiselled into the stone above the chimney piece, its origins go back to the middle of the eighteenth century when the ruling Archduke of Tuscany, Pietro Leopoldo, made tax concessions to encourage the people

ABOVE *The traditional 1750s* casa colonica, *or farmhouse, with its covered loggia and square central tower.*

ABOVE LEFT *These angel-like figures are chiselled from poplar trees.*

LEFT *The karge terracotta figures by Matthew keep silent watch beneath the shade of the cypress trees.*

BELOW *The view over Chianti's famous wine lands and hillside of holm oak, chestnut and pine trees.*

who worked the land to build houses. In the 1960s, after the end of the *mezzadria*, the feudal system of farming, many of these farmhouses were left abandoned as the peasants, or *contadini*, became salaried workers and migrated to the city. As they moved out, foreigners, the English in particular, moved in.

The Spenders have chosen a self-sufficient lifestyle, which exists in close harmony with the traditions and natural rhythms of the land, a lifestyle not so different from the Tuscan *contadini* farmers whose "agricultural duties are shaped by habits that go back to Roman times, punctuated not so much by the seasons as by the changing moon and recurring name days of saints" (*Within Tuscany*).

It is Maro who tends the garden, a passion she compares to painting. "The intention is to create order out of chaos, yet it's exciting when things don't go as you plan and the medium

ABOVE *A mosaic portrait of Maro by her godmother, American artist Jeanne Reynald, hangs in the dining room. Maro made all the decorative majolica on display. The white sculpture is by Matthew, the marble from the Greek island Paros.*

RIGHT *In daughter Saskia's bedroom, sculptures by Matthew decorate an alcove next to a Tuscan empire sofa and a chest crafted by Matthew and decorated by Maro.*

96

LEFT *This corner of the bathroom is set up as a personal shrine of family mementoes and memorabilia. The shell collage is by Maro, the gold votive hand by Matthew, and the Sicilian tambourine was a holiday souvenir.*

RIGHT *Saskia's bedroom has been newly repainted using a mix of natural powder pigment, wallpaper, glue and water in a happy shade of green, balanced by the warm pink of tinted brickwork and a silk bedspread.*

BELOW *This is a self-sufficient household where Matthew is the carpenter who makes all the bedframes, and Maro embellishes all the surfaces, such as the bed and cupboard in the bedroom, with her free-spirited, exuberant designs.*

itself answers back." So she wages a daily battle against the galloping euphorbia, fennel and rosemary, and then retires to her studio to regain control over her unfinished canvases. All the food they eat they grow themselves; the wine, the rocket, tomatoes and olive oil in the salad at lunch, the eggs for breakfast.

The self-sufficiency extends to life within the house as well, where everything – furniture, artwork, even the bricks and mortar framework – has been crafted by them. Matthew is the carpenter; the sinuous staircase that curls like a nautilus shell from the dining room up to the bedrooms was carved by him from *pietra serena*, the blue-grey stone extracted from local Florentine quarries. Having spent eight months in Carrara, where Michelangelo sculpted, extracting the stone from the mountain, he is obsessed with this medium. "He is the sort of person," says Maro, "who will come back from a holiday in Greece not with a straw hat or cheerful souvenir, but with a couple of tons of rock in his suitcase." Maro's own exuberant beaded designs embellish mirrors, crockery, tiles, cupboards and bed-heads. It is a decorative style that deflates pomposity. Discarded antlers found on the lawn have worked their way into

a chandelier fashioned by Matthew. These have become the wings of a fanciful Chagallian flying figure suspended from the ceiling by a crystal necklace, with head and arms as candle supports. And nearby, a gaudy gilded palm tree lamp stands somewhat incongruously next to a fine oil painting. "We found it in a Florentine market, and introduced it to prevent the house becoming too tasteful."

The whimsical aesthetics of the furnishings and the bantering freedom of the conversation are part of the free-spirited irreverence of the Spender-Gorky household. Here, the chickens cavort in frescoed palaces, canaries sing in gilded cages and peacocks strut around the tabletop debris of a long alfresco lunch. Impromptu guests take their siesta beneath the shade of the fat mulberry tree on the lawn or by the tree-lined swimming pool. The film director Bernardo Bertolucci, a family friend, was so taken with this peculiarly English version of a Tuscan idyll that he turned it into a film. A memento of *Stealing Beauty*, in the shape of a cedar carving of the actress Liv Tyler, still stands amid the silent terracotta army of sculptures by Spender at the front of the house.

ARNIANO
TUSCANY

JASPER AND
CAMILLA GUINNESS

ABOVE *Arniano, standing full
square against the elements.*

LEFT *Limewashed walls and natural
terracotta and flagstone floors create
an uncontrived, simple style.*

BELOW *Camilla with daughters
Amber and Claudia.*

To the south-east of Siena, the familiar Tuscan countryside becomes less garden-like, tidy and contained. The chalky uplands of the Sienese *crete* roll away to meet wider horizons, denuded but for the occasional stark silhouettes of a spine of cypresses and wheels of wheat. On the edge of this great agricultural expanse, well off the beaten track, is the house of Jasper and Camilla Guinness and their children.

Once off the asphalt, a rough track follows a slow, twisting ascent through thick copses of oak and chestnut that curves, eventually, into a drive of adolescent cypresses and lavender hedges. A house with pale blue shutters, dripping with banksia roses and wisteria, suggests an English sensibility. But the foundations belong to a typical sturdy Tuscan farmhouse, a *casa colonica*, standing full square against the elements, with the land dropping away on all sides.

It was the wilderness and remoteness of the place that seduced the recently wedded couple some ten years ago. Jasper was lecturing at the British Institute in Florence after leaving university in England and never looked back. By chance he and Camilla came across Arniano, a house in the middle of nowhere but with generous views over the valleys to distant hills crowned with the castles of the local gentry.

"The building had no distinguishing beauty apart from what the landscape brings to it," says Jasper. "It was a roofless ruin, but inside we could see the potential; here was space, light, high ceilings, generous proportions – a rare thing in a Tuscan farmhouse. And not a single poky room."

So they moved in, accompanied by a baby daughter and a host of builders and the few paltry contents of their household. The only habitable room in the house was a central *salotto* on the floor directly above the old manger. This would have been the main living quarters of the

ABOVE *Desmond Guinness, a relative, gave Jasper the* arazzo finto, *which is not a tapestry but a hanging on painted canvas. The steel and brick beams of the drawing room are peculiar to the farmhouses of this area. The cushions are from Camilla's shop.*

RIGHT *The landscapes on the walls are by Kenya-based painter David Marrion from a series of snapshots taken by Camilla. A canvas by Spanish artist Ana Corvero hangs above a plate by James Campbell.*

RIGHT *Light floods into the drawing room, which once housed the stables. Camilla Guinness's talent as an interior designer lies in her eye for a bargain and a taste for comfort. These furnishings have been transformed from the most basic materials – an inexpensive enamel jug stands on an old electricity-cable wheel found discarded in a field, while second-hand linen sheets have been made into curtains.*

LEFT *Another example of thriftshop chic: this corner of the kitchen with its welcoming open hearth is decorated with old ginger beer bottles and a metal ventilator screen bought from an English market.*

FAR LEFT *Jasper's study is colourwashed in burnt orange, with photographs of William Acton's drawings of the Mitford sisters.*

contadini, or local peasant farmers, with the warmth from the huddled livestock below providing natural central heating. It now doubles as a children's den and television room. But as a legacy of those makeshift days, daughter Amber still carries a scar from a workman's wayward chisel.

Gradually, however, the original haybarn was converted into a pool house. They levelled out the sloping floors in the original stables and converted the space into an airy drawing room with french windows on both sides.

Beyond this is the kitchen, the hub of the house, with one wall dominated by an open raised fireplace for cooking. The wall opposite is completely taken over by a large storage cupboard made by their friend Charles Carr from reclaimed wood and bricks. Light floods into the room from windows embracing views over the corduroy-hills and from glass doors opening onto a walled garden, which is Jasper's labour of love. The high-level windows on either side of the fireplace were one of the most costly additions to the building, installed at the recommendation of their friend, renowned interior decorator Teddy Millington Drake. "We then cursed him for the expense but, of course, he was right – they help to make this the lightest room in the house."

Camilla may lament the fact that the kitchen, with its open fire, has to be repainted every six months and that it gathers dust but, equally, it gathers people, too. Guests tend to congregate here throughout the day, attracted by the enticing smells of cooking. Having worked briefly in the kitchens of London's acclaimed River Café restaurant, Camilla is an expert cook, adept at improvising dishes out of fresh produce from the markets and her garden. At one recent lunch

ABOVE *The kitchen opens onto a walled herb garden.*

LEFT AND RIGHT *In the five bedrooms the furnishings and decoration are kept pared down. There are no paintings, only simple wooden and metal bed-heads and diaphanous drapes that do not detract from the spectacular views.*

FAR RIGHT *One of these metal bed-heads once belonged to Gore Vidal.*

party for forty friends, she made it all look easy. Dish upon dish materialize, apparently out of nowhere; roast pork with prunes and pine nuts, pasta with fresh mint from the garden, Tuscan lentil stews, home-made bread toasted on the embers for bruschetta. Life at Arniano seductively combines the spirit of spontaneous conviviality that is part of the Italian *art de vivre*, with the unpretentious relaxed comfort that is the essence of an English country house.

If effortless, uncontrived elegance is the hallmark of the Guinness hospitality, the interiors and the decorative style reflect it. Camilla owns a shop in neighbouring Buonconvento filled with fine fabrics and objects. When she wants to dress things up (or down) in her own home, objects from her shop – a chandelier, lantern, a swathe of velvet – find themselves migrating to Arniano. It is a house that is constantly evolving; surface decoration, trinkets and fabrics change with the seasons, with the occasion and with the mood.

Fabrics are her particular weakness: toile de Jouy from markets in France, velvets from England, lace from Italy, Irish cottons and linens, silks from India. These inject colour and add a sense of the theatrical to an otherwise neutral, mostly whitewashed backdrop. "A single length of fabric can be so versatile" – sometimes used as a tablecloth or bedcover, sometimes draped at a window for curtains, sometimes wrapped around her own shoulders.

Although several Italians have commissioned Camilla to decorate their homes, she insists her talents as a designer stem from her eye for a bargain and a taste for comfort. The locally made sofas, are deep and squashy and strewn with cushions. Even the guest bathroom boasts a chaise longue that invites lounging. The sense of easy luxury comes not only from the comfortable arrangement of the space and furniture, and in the attention to good food and wine, but also from the smaller details. Beds boast several pillows dressed in ironed Irish cotton, towels are so white and huge they trail behind you like a bridal train. Full bottles of Floris oil and scented candles stand beside the hot tap.

In the five bedrooms, the furnishings and decoration are kept studiously pared down – a few paintings, simple metal bed-heads and white diaphanous drapes to avoid detracting from the spectacular panoramic views, which are a decorative statement in themselves.

LE FONTANELLE
TUSCANY

PIERO CASTELLINI

YOU SPY IT WELL BEFORE YOU REACH IT: the solid symmetry of the Tuscan farmhouse on the road south from Montalcino, terracotta roof grazed by a line of cypresses, its feet rooted in the endless sloping ranks of vines, which unfurl into the quivering distance like a bolt of green corduroy.

In midsummer, the fierce-as-a-lion sun, or *il sol leone*, as it is called in these parts, turns the fields the colour of bronze. Le Fontanelle (little fountains) – the house of designer Piero Castellini – does not always live up to its name. People move languorously as the barometer hits forty-five degrees and a sirocco wind blows as hot and dry as a hairdryer from the sea thirty kilometres away. "They even suspend court cases when the sirocco blows," says Castellini, "No one functions properly." However, immaculate in linen, he looks quite the opposite of a man who ever wilts in the heat. A successful architect, designer and decorator from Milan, he is a man of hyperactive enthusiasms, juggling his textiles industry with a museum in honour of his grandfather, the renowned architect Piero Portalupo, and a dozen different work projects abroad.

Le Fontanelle, a converted farmhouse and estate in the province of Siena, is where he comes to escape the pressures of city life and work. Even here, his energies are absorbed by the challenge of converting a couple of outlying ruined outhouses into sumptuous villas to rent, but being active helps him to relax. "I enjoy the rhythm of country life, the early morning and evening rides galloping across wide, open landscape without gates and fences. I like the congenial background orchestra of people: villagers, builders, gardeners, farmers dropping in for gossip, dispensing advice, offering help." Le Fontanelle is a place where, more than anywhere else, he breathes easily.

Indeed, the sense of peace Le Fontanelle exudes is almost tangible. Nothing jars, nothing is out of place. Even Ash, the resident blond Weimaraner dog, and the terracotta-coloured cat

ABOVE LEFT AND ABOVE
Castellini and also Le Fontanelle, with its traditional square and solid structure set above vineyards.

LEFT *In the covered loggia, Castellini has tempered the integral rusticity of the structure by commissioning Adam Alvarez to paint the walls in stripes of sky-blue. The wine, fruit and bowls are all locally grown and made.*

ABOVE AND LEFT *The natural austerity of the architecture is softened by the warm terracotta wash of the walls and an array of climbing plants and roses, including "Mermaid" over the arched trellis. The Napoleonic camp lantern in the loggia was restored by Castellini, who also designed the table and chairs. Spherical objects are a recurring decorative motif, seen here in a display of ornamental stone balls.*

RIGHT *Geraniums cascade from a collection of Mediterranean urns and old olive oil jars on the terrace. The terracotta paving is nineteenth century and was fortuitously discovered in a nearby pig barn.*

LEFT *The cherrywood sofa is covered in toile de Jouy by Bourger, and the chaise longue is upholstered in a fabric from Castellini's own textile company, C&C designs in Milan. Despite the refinement of the furnishings, these interiors are never ostentatious – the beamed ceiling is left unplastered and a simple muslin drape frames the window.*

RIGHT *Against the powdery backdrop of colourwashed walls, Castellini displays an eclectic group of objects chosen not only for their colour, which reflect the soothing lavender shade of the walls, but also for their pleasing texture and shape. The oval frames above the mantelpiece in the bedroom are eighteenth-century plaster cameos from Piedmont. En masse, even such humble objects as the walking sticks have a decorative resonance that goes beyond their practical purpose.*

match the honeyed hues of the stuccoed exterior. Nature is always the starting point for Castellini's decorative scheme. The building has been washed in terracotta, the colour that most evocatively captures the feel of Italy and harmonizes with the warm earth tones of the land. Inside, mellow distempered walls reflect the yellow of a field of sunflowers. Upstairs the palette runs through a spectrum of sky-blues, from the duck-egg pallor of the Tuscan horizon at high noon to the dusty lilac of twilight.

Against this powdery backdrop of colourwashed walls, Castellini displays an eclectic group of objects gleaned from frequent trips around the world. These are not necessarily valuable, and sometimes they have been chosen simply for their pleasing textures and the purity of their shapes. Globes and spheres sound a recurring note, from the cannon balls in the garden to the strategically placed stone orbs on the staircase and the display of old metal boules used in the game of *pétanque*. In the living rooms, intriguing collections of antique architectural tools, callipers and mechanical instruments inherited from his architect grandfather help furnish the space. "If I see something I like, an old hunting horn, an old leather suitcase, I can't buy just one of it – I buy the lot and turn it into a collection." And the decorative impact of the house comes not so much from the objects themselves but in Castellini's talent for displaying them so they complement each other and command attention. Thus, even the humble and practical instruments of daily life, such as the cluster of rustic watering cans and walking sticks in the hall, are imbued with all the visual impact of a still life.

When he acquired the farmhouse, Castellini chose to strip the building down to its bare bones and used natural materials that mellow with time, such as terracotta tiles and a seagrass matting of his own design. He left the graceful vaulted ceilings unplastered and allowed the patina of age to show on the unpolished wooden beams of the bedroom ceilings. "A country house should grow into itself. I bought Le Fontanelle fifteen years ago and believe that, like wine, it improves over the passing years. Above all I wanted truth of colour, form and texture. The architecture of the farmhouse, with its sloping sturdy outer walls, its square proportions and solidity, has a resonance all of its own. I wanted to retain this honesty of form and celebrate, within the house, the true intensity of the colour that you see in the landscape around you." There is a sobriety and an authenticity to these interiors, which is never ostentatious, despite the refinement of the furniture where Chinese colonial chests, neoclassical chairs and statuary and Louis XVI tables intermingle.

Castellini describes his style as fundamentally minimalist and his temperament as traditionalist. As a designer, he says, you take the best aspects of the past and make them your own. "Copying can be an art form in itself." So the outlying land is treated with the same respect for the past as are the building's foundations. He has followed ancient agricultural practices and planted up the soil with alternating rows of vines and olives, three lines of vine to one of olive. The garden is a passion, a sensual profusion of aromatic herbs – thyme, sage, lemon verbena and citronella. Plumbago and delicate "Mermaid" climbing roses tumble romantically over pergolas, bowers and the walls of an enclosed orchard. But sometimes the extremes of the Tuscan climate can defeat even his controlling energy and best-laid plans – but then, as he says, it is always the idea of the challenge to which he responds and which inspires him.

ABOVE *The kitchen-dining room reveals unplastered terracotta vaulted ceiling, unwaxed floor tiles and warm, colourwashed walls.*

LEFT *In the drawing room a harpsichord displays a collection of marble globes (above left) that sound a recurring note, as well as a neoclassical bust (below left). The chair and plaster bas relief are eighteenth century northern Italian.*

117

CALCATA
LAZIO

STEFANO MASSIMO

ABOVE *Stefano Massimo and his English wife, Helen.*

ABOVE LEFT *Calcata, the medieval citadel, sits perched above the Treia gorge.*

LEFT *The Roman jacuzzi-bath, theatrically screened off from the entrance hall with velvet drapes, was once the oven in the village bakery. The tub itself is carved from a piece of red marble, its base an intricate mosaic in gold and lapis lazuli.*

North of Rome, the campagna Romana stretches from the Sabine Hills to the Tyrrhenian sea, concealing a landscape of lakes born from the craters of long-extinct volcanoes, of plains broken by deep wooded gorges, ravines and craggy precipices crowned here and there with ancient Roman and medieval ruins. The strange melancholy of these perspectives and the suffused light haunted the artists of the Romantic era – painters like Claude, Corot and Poussin who captured the solitude and dishevelled wilderness of this land in oils.

Once, however, centuries before Christ, this region of northern Lazio, the Etruria of antiquity, was the richest and most densely populated corner of the peninsula. Invading Roman armies effectively wiped out the Etruscan civilization, and later the territory became a figurative chessboard in the struggles for supremacy among the leading papal families. Well-fortified castles and villas were built as competing symbols of wealth for the new Roman elite.

One such stronghold is Calcata, a perfect medieval citadel perched on a spur high above the gurgling Treia valley gorge, a sleeping-beauty castle cloaked in a tangle of hazelnut leaf and ivy, juniper and holm oak. For four centuries it passed back and forth in a power match between the Sinibaldi and Anguillara families until 1828, when it fell into the hands of a branch of the Massimo family, one of the oldest dynasties of the Roman papal aristocracy.

After the death of the last male heir at the beginning of the twentieth century, the community began to break up. Calcata might have been abandoned altogether and left to tumble into ruin had not a wave of New Age artists and hippies claimed it in the 1970s. Now Romans visit in their droves at weekends to admire the artists' handicrafts and imbibe the mystical beauty of the place. The narrow passages of the walled village-fortress are accessible only to those on foot. A dark steep alleyway ascends to a second imposing gateway, which opens onto the

LEFT *Much of the grandeur of these interiors is influenced by the quality of the materials, the different marbles, fine stone and terracotta, which provide the architectural framework.*

RIGHT *The decorative effect of the chair and drapes is even more opulent when set against the simplicity of white limewash and terracotta. The French leather chair was found in an antique shop in London; the velvet cushion and curtain from Judy Greenwood in London have been chosen for their rich texture and colour.*

FAR RIGHT *Massimo has created a sense of grandeur within this clifftop dwelling, placing great emphasis on its structural elements – the floors, ceilings, staircases and architraves. For this room, he commissioned a local sculptor to craft the Romanesque-style twisted pillars of the fireplace from volcanic tufa stone.*

piazza. Beyond this, a cobbled street traces the edge of the battlements to the entrance of Stefano Massimo's home.

An energetic London-based photographer and distant descendant of the noble Massimo family that once held feudal control over the village, Stefano was familiar with Calcata from childhood excursions with his Etruscologist father. On the hunt for a weekend retreat for himself and Helen, his English wife, he found Calcata, which seemed to fulfil all his criteria. Within an hour's driving distance of Rome, here was unspoilt country where wild boar still roamed, where hawks soared on thermals, with limpid lakes and hot springs to swim in.

Nestling against the bastions of the village-fortress, Massimo's house seems to grow out of the rock that supports it. The space, which had once included the village bakery and a warren of cave dwellings housing livestock and farm machinery, has now been linked with a maze of corridors and intricate staircases that connect the different levels. Yet this is by no means a humble troglodyte lodging. Despite the smallness of the rooms, the uneven bumps and lumps of the plastered walls, which have been literally hewn out of the soft tufa rock face, the effect is of a grand and noble residence. Massimo has counteracted the integral rusticity of the space by paying particular attention to the architectural framework.

Marble is his passion, and he rifled quarries for the finest stone. The elegant twisting staircases were sculpted out of the milky travertine marble, the most popular building stone of Rome for centuries. The architraves around windows and doorways are fashioned out of the rough-textured, ashen-grey peperino rock quarried from the Alban Hills south of the capital. The sink in the main bathroom is a solid piece of red rosso antico marble from Verona. He also pored over

architectural designs of Roman villas and followed ancient building techniques to construct the most remarkable feature of the house, a mosaicked Roman circular jacuzzi-bath with a terracotta brick ceiling adapted from the beehive-dome of what was formerly the baker's oven. The intricacy of the ceiling and mosaic work is bought to life by the shifting light of candles. Screened off with velvet curtains, this feels like a superbly decadent corner of imperial Rome.

In the adjacent drawing room, a rich seventeenth-century embroidered drape across the entrance wall, displaying the crest of his ancestor Cardinal Camillo Massimo, further accentuates the grand imperial tone in this, the largest room of the house. The red of the hanging is picked up in a kilim by George Smith, used to cover the custom-made circular sofa, and in the rich jewel-tones of the chair and curtain fabrics. Here, as in the other rooms, is a strong, confident decorative scheme that works strikingly well within the unconventional framework of the house. The sumptuous furnishings embrace even the most awkward nooks and crannies, and give a sense of unity to the maze of interconnecting spaces.

"I wanted to create an idea of luxury and elegance, although with no true corners the rooms were actually quite a challenge to furnish," explains Massimo. He enthusiastically extols the

perks and comforts of living in a cave: "warm, cosy and perfect for hibernating in the winter, and yet blissfully cool in the summer". There is no sense of claustrophobia either, Massimo insists, for although many of the rooms are embedded in the rock face, the dramatic views over the ravine from every window, and the infinite perspectives, give a sense of exhilarating freedom. This is perhaps why he seems to take most delight in the outdoor shower room, positioned on a vertiginous terrace wedged into a cleft in the cliff-face.

"To shower, alfresco, overlooked by no one, against the eternal sound of the gushing river, a river that never dries out even in the height of summer, is about as liberating and sybaritic a sensation as you can have," he says – just part of the unusual experience of living on the craggy rooftop of this ancient landscape, in a house that is, at once, eagle's nest, cave, grand seigneurial residence and a unique medieval fortress-home.

ABOVE *The copper bath and fixtures are nineteenth-century English and have been aged further with acid. Terracotta tiles from neighbouring Orvieto have been laid in an intricate patchwork design. The walls are a mixture of limewash and natural powder pigment bought in Rome.*

RIGHT *An elegant Indo-Portuguese four-poster bed; the floor was lowered a few inches to accommodate it.*

CASA PAGANI
PUGLIA

AMEDEO PAGANI

AFTER THE DRAMATIC, ALMOST LUNAR landscape of neighbouring Basilicata, with its staccato peaks and troughs, the road into Puglia, in the heel of Italy, stretches languorously ahead, rising and falling over gentle hills as regularly as a heartbeat. Its dry soil has been cultivated assiduously – vineyards, orchards and olive groves are neatly stitched together with a crisscross of low drystone walls. This is landscape on a more intimate scale. Even the architecture is playful, from the exuberance of the towns' baroque churches and palazzi, which cheerfully break all the rules of classical restraint, to the pepperpot-shaped houses known as *trulli*, unique to the region and more particularly to the Itria valley.

The road continues ever southwards, past the sleeping beauty that is the city of Lecce, the Florence of the south. In the middle of the afternoon it is shuttered up. An empty, silent place, it stirs to life only when the churches reopen at five. This is the Salentine peninsula, the narrowest part of Italy, at the very tip of the heel. And somewhere amid the endless acres of ancient and gnarled olive groves is the house of Amedeo Pagani. The much travelled former anthropologist, now a writer and a successful player in the Italian film industry (he wrote *The Night Porter* and produced the award-winning film *In the Mood for Love*), has chosen this forgotten, unfashionable corner of the country for his summer retreat.

The approach to the house, down a long and dusty track, is announced by a high wall. There is nothing to give away the fact that people live here but a modest door in the brickwork. This opens onto a secret garden and a paved terrace along which, sheltering under a bower of vines, is a low, single-storeyed lodging. The blond stone façade with pale blue louvred doors reveals nothing of the exoticism within. Pagani and his former partner Nicoletta extended this former eighteenth-century roadside chapel laterally, building a series

ABOVE Relaxed alfresco dinners take place on the vine-covered terrace.

LEFT Louvred shutters and a simple staircase carved from local soft stone embellish the façade. The stairs lead to an open roof terrace where Pagani sometimes sleeps on warm nights.

BELOW Amedeo Pagani on the terrace of his home.

of interconnecting spaces, which make up the kitchen, three bedrooms and bathrooms. He refers to the rooms as his "cells"; with their thick stone walls, and small windows, they are a sanctuary from the heat by day.

Yet the general stylistic effect and atmosphere of the house are anything but ascetic. The decoration of the chapel, now his living room, is audacious and flamboyant. The ornate altarpiece decorated in the style of southern Baroque, with stucco scrolls and curlicues intact, now crowns the hearth. Pagani has exploited the inherent theatricality of the room with its original vaulted ceilings by painting the walls cardinal red. He built up the colours in layers to bring depth and intensity to the surface using a mix of glue paste and natural powder pigments, bought in a humble ironmonger's in Rome. The ornaments are spare and simple: a Tibetan singing bowl, prayer stools, antique Neapolitan maritime lanterns, palm fronds from the

ABOVE *The interior is a lateral conversion of open, interconnecting spaces making up the kitchen (shown with a view into the living room), bathrooms and three bedrooms. Small windows and four-feet thick walls offer a cool sanctuary from the heat of the day.*

RIGHT *The ornate stucco altarpiece crowns a fireplace in the living room, originally a roadside chapel, while the walls are painted cardinal red.*

LEFT *While furnishings are sparse and simple, the true drama of these interiors comes from the play of sunlight on the walls, which changes by the hour, highlighting the different patina and textures of the tinted plaster. Pagani built up the colours in layers to bring depth and intensity to the surface using a mix of glue paste and natural powder pigments.*

RIGHT AND LEFT *Simplicity is the key to interiors that boast a relaxed, natural decorative style, including palm fronds from the garden and a bowl of fruit grown in the owner's orchard.*

garden – minimal furnishings so as not to detract from the true drama of the house, which is the play of sunlight on the walls.

The light changes by the hour, subtly altering the moods and illuminating the different patina and texture of the plastered walls. Throughout the house, the walls have been washed a rainbow spectrum of colour: there is green for the bathroom, burnt sienna for the kitchen, blue in a cloakroom. "Verde Veronese, cerulo, azzurro," Pagani chants. He explains that the roots of this passion go back to a childhood spent in Eritrea and Ethiopia, parched lands where colour is as refreshing, and perhaps as necessary, to the senses as a glass of cold water. Only the master bedroom, once orange, has reverted back to virginal white as Pagani found the hue so vibrant it prevented sleep.

He continues to travel constantly, most recently making films in Argentina and Europe. Being on the move and living in the city, usually Rome or Paris, he says that "Life becomes full of people and clutter. Here, in Puglia, it is all about paring things down to the bare essentials.

I surround myself with my family and the friends I care about, and I love to potter around. In the process, I rediscover myself."

Alfresco lunches and the pleasurable rituals of summer revolve around the vine-covered terrace table, once used by estate workers for sorting tobacco leaves. "Most appropriate," he says, "for I smoke like a trooper." On hot nights Pagani might sleep on the roof or shower in the garden. He has also adapted the hollowed-out trunk of an ancient fig tree into a magical outdoor den softened with cushions. In the evening he makes a habit of driving to one of the deserted beaches, all within a fifteen-mile drive on this narrow peninsula, to watch the magical sunsets.

"I like the extremity of this part of Italy. It is truly a land's end, *Finibus Terrae*, empty and wild. I like the authenticity of the lifestyle here, the aromatic intensity of the wine and food. Most Romans cannot conceive the point of a summer retreat that is close to, but not directly on the sea, and Puglia 'in the godforsaken south' is still, in their minds, the back of beyond. I say, long may it stay that way."

LEFT AND BELOW LEFT *With plain whitewashed walls, an undressed window and a bed made from a mattress wedged in a built-in concrete platform, Pagani's bedroom feels almost cell-like. However, a collection of Eritrean pots and colourful wooden toys and towers, made locally in the town of Maglie and displayed along the bed-head and in the alcove shelving, adds a playful and purely decorative note to counter any sense of asceticism.*

ABOVE RIGHT AND RIGHT *The master bathroom, with panels painted in various shades of veronese green, has a style that is both sophisticated and uncontrived. While Pagani likes to describe his house as a series of interconnecting cells, the mood and dramatic interest of these interiors are varied by the changing colours of the stuccoed walls. The basin has been sunk into a distressed pine dressing table found locally, and a harvester's basket, once used for collecting grapes, serves as a wastepaper bin.*

CASA SERVADIO
STROMBOLI

GAIA SERVADIO

IT IS THE HOUR BEFORE DUSK ON THE Sicilian island of Stromboli. This is the magic hour when the heat of the day has abated and the wind settles down.

Gaia Servadio, the writer and part-time islander, calls it *l'heure bleue*, the time to give the garden and then her guests a drink. Verdi is blasting out from the stereo, and she whistles as she waters, pointing proudly at her basil that was planted only a month ago and is now already brushing her knees. Everything grows as fast as Jack's beanstalk in this rich volcanic soil. The lemons, which she collects to go with tonight's fish couscous, are as big as melons. Chores done, Gaia uncorks a bottle of malvasia, the local wine, and sits with friends on the rooftop terrace at the foot of the volcano and watches the sun sink into the sea. The last rays bump against the dark flank of the volcano, bruising it pink, violet, and then purple. The volcano, or *Iddu* as the locals call it, towers to nearly one thousand metres and defines the atmosphere and the landscape of this island. It makes the beaches charcoal-dark, and carpets the slopes with grasses of a fluorescent green. Even the wine evokes its brooding presence – the malvasia that French writer Guy de Maupassant dubbed *le vin du diable*, or devil's wine, tastes of earth and sulphur.

At regular intervals the volcano growls and spits and coughs up magma and debris. On clear nights you can see the explosions like brilliant party streamers cascading from the summit. By day it seems more benign, resembling something from a Magritte painting – a surrealist bowler-hatted giant puffing quietly on a cigarette, as the writer Alan Ross describes it in his book about the islands, *Reflections on Blue Water*.

Gaia, who is proud of her Sicilian blood, fell in love with Stromboli some years ago and bought a house here, seduced not only by its wine-dark seas and by the undeniable drama of the landscape but by the unchanging simplicity of the villagers' lifestyle. There are no cars, no street lamps and no bank, and sometimes the place is cut off from the mainland, like the other

ABOVE *Gaia Servadio at the table where friends regularly congregate.*

ABOVE LEFT *Wall tiles depicting citrus fruit, the symbol of the island, are made by Allegra Mostyn Owen.*

LEFT *The owner's hammock hangs next to scented jasmine bushes and beneath a bougainvillaea tree.*

BELOW *A view of the exterior, in traditional blue and white.*

ABOVE *All the rooms open onto this central covered courtyard, following a tradition that goes back to Mycenean antiquity. The dining "room" repeats the blue and white theme of island architecture. The tile-covered benches called* bisole *are part of the classical architectural lexicon of the Aeolian archipelago. The painting is by Servadio's son.*

LEFT *A Sicilian candlestick and fruit from the garden.*

136

islands that form the Aeolian chain, by a turbulent ocean and fierce winds. It is no coincidence that the Ancient Greeks believed the islands to be the home of Aeolus, the god of the winds, who gave the archipelago its name. And, despite the glamour of its most famous residents – the director Roberto Rossellini lived here with Ingrid Bergman during the shooting of the film *Stromboli* in the 1950s – the island has resisted the influx of the glitterati who have chosen to build their holiday homes in neighbouring Panarea instead.

Gaia's island retreat is built in the traditional Aeolian architectural style. It is a basic whitewashed collection of rooms in *pietra morta* – lava-stone cemented with mortar mixed with lime – surrounding an internal garden. The structure is cubic and flat-roofed to withstand continuous seismic tremors and to facilitate the collection of precious rainwater from earthenware urns set at each corner. Converted from wine vats and a stable, Gaia's home now boasts three

ABOVE *A characteristically unself-conscious still life of everyday objects: weathered table, broom and giant citrus waiting to be turned into marmalade. The framed oil painting of Provence is by Gaia's son, Orlando Mostyn Owen. The Milanese ceramic jelly moulds are the only extravagance, a present from regular guest Inge Feltrinelli. The destructive effects of pumice dust and sea air dictate minimal and basic furnishings; here, a length of cotton lace serves as a simple curtain.*

ABOVE *The traditional whitewashed cubic buildings have been constructed to withstand seismic tremors. The flat roof, accessed by an external staircase, makes an ideal terrace for cocktails; it looks out over the sea and the flanks of the one-hundred-thousand-year-old volcano.*

ABOVE *Servadio is a passionate collector of Italian ceramics, which she believes, immediately furnish a home, like books. The cachepot from Santo Stefano di Camastra in Sicily is typical eighteenth-century. The tin bowl is a market find from the neighbouring island of Lipari.*

bedrooms and two bathrooms and a sitting room to accommodate any spillover of people, books and CDs. But life really takes place in the shaded garden, which has been divided up into a patchwork of outside "rooms" for dozing during the siesta hour, reading, dining and cooking.

A wide terrace covered by a bower of cane sticks supported on pillars, or *pulera*, runs the length of the building. In local dialect, this covered terrace is the *bagghiu*, and it covers an area that serves as Gaia's outdoor kitchen where the old bread oven still smoulders. It provides shelter for her collection of straw hats and walking sticks and the resident gecko. "They keep mosquitoes away," she says approvingly.

The low stone walls that separate the *bagghiu* from the dining area beneath the vines have been covered in tiles to form traditional tiled benches called *bisole*. This enclosure forms the hub of the house. Beyond this, on one side, is a raised vegetable plot, and on the other, an open garden overflowing with hibiscus, geranium and jasmine, amid which doves like to coo and strut. Gaia's own favourite spot is the siesta-hammock strung out between the junk room and the old stable. Another corner of the garden, adjacent to a miniature lemon grove, has been paved over to form an informal sitting room, with parasols, oil lamps, cane furniture and cushions festooned across the built-in benches. This area metamorphoses into a wonderful alfresco dining room at night, with open views over the smouldering volcano and the canopy of stars.

The fine grey pumice dust from the volcano covers everything, and the salty sea air is corrosive, so furnishings and decoration both inside and out are kept simple. A length of lace

RIGHT *The* bagghiu, *or covered terrace, is a traditional feature of Aeolian architecture, with a bower of local reed or cane to provide shade. Beyond the low stone wall is a small vegetable garden edged with potted basil to deter mosquitoes. The outdoor sink is decorated in southern Italian style with handmade tiles, and there is a wood-burning oven built into the low wall.*

LEFT *The flotsam of daily life and more valuable objects are given equal prominence in Gaia's house. Here a framed print of the Last Judgement in the* salotto *hangs above a simple farmhouse chair. Open shelves hold a collection of important classics and local pottery, all helping to furnish the room.*

RIGHT *The master bedroom opens onto the garden and the living room. The framed watercolours depict the saga of Don Quixote and were a present from a friend, Chilean-French artist Matta. The bedspread is another present from Inge Feltrinelli, and the church candleholder, used during frequent power failures, is seventeenth-century Italian.*

strung onto a bamboo pole serves as a curtain and keeps away the flying insects. Odd bits of jumble – a polished stone, a few interesting beads, a sculptural piece of driftwood, a couple of shells, all of which have at some stage attracted Gaia's magpie eye – clamour for equal attention next to some of her more valuable pieces – original prints by artist friends like Matta, Guttuso and Adami, and antique and modern ceramics gleaned from trips to Puglia, Ripa Bianca in Umbria and Caltagirone in Sicily.

Her son Orlando Mostyn Owen's and her own paintings also decorate the walls. Although writing now takes up most of her time, she was once a painter too, not to mention a broadcaster and arts correspondent for Italy's premier daily *Corriere della Sera*. Having spent over thirty years in England, now enjoying her second marriage to an Englishman and with houses and a busy career and social life in London, Rome and Umbria, Gaia is happy to retreat to her little house in Stromboli, which make so few demands on her and requires minimal upkeep. Happy to come alone, if necessary, several times a year to work on her writing, happy to concoct more spontaneous recipes from the produce in her garden, happy to wake up with the doves and listen to the garden humming with insects drunk on the nectar. She suggests that in buying this house she has not only recreated the idyllic, uncomplicated holidays of her youth by the seaside in Lerici but is also preparing for old age. "There is a wonderful little cemetery up the hill which is completely tiled – that's where I want to end up," she claims. In the meantime, the daily dips in the cleanest, most limpid sea in the Mediterranean continue to invigorate. "The sulphuric air, the unspoilt charm of the people, the local food and wine – these are the luxuries that mean most to me, the things that make me feel positively well."

IL MONASTERO
PANTELLERIA

FABRIZIO FERRI

MAROONED IN THE TURBULENT straits between Sicily and Tunisia, Pantelleria is a blackened outcrop of an island, blasted by sirocco winds that blow hot from the Sahara and collide with the cooler mistral from the north. There are no beaches, only sheer cliffs and jagged basalt bays that have names like *Cinque Denti* or "five teeth" – names that conjure up the ruggedness of this volcanic coastline.

It doesn't actually always feel like Italy. The four hundred years of Moorish domination left an indelible mark and the island, which lies only seventy kilometres from the coast of Tunisia, retains a distinct north African flavour. Arab words linger in the local dialect and define important place names. The word Pantelleria is itself a corruption of the Arabic *Bent el Rhia*, meaning "daughter of the winds".

The Moors were by inclination farmers rather than fisherman; they introduced the citrus, the date palm and the prickly pear. They protected their orchards and citrus groves against the elements behind high-walled circular gardens that are still to be found dotted across the terraced plains. Fearful of pirates and the unpredictable sea, they turned their backs on the coast and built windowless houses, called *dammusi*, facing inland. The sturdy cubic structure and domed roof of the *dammuso* is a unique feature of the Pantellerian scenery. Constructed from unplastered lava stone – the volcanic debris that lies scattered across the land – the dwellings blend seamlessly into the rocky terrain. So great is their camouflage that Fabrizio Ferri, the renowned fashion photographer and entrepreneur, spent weeks admiring and wandering through the fields of vines and caper bushes on the foot hills of the volcano before he detected the presence of a ruined clutch of rustic dwellings – the five *dammusi* that would eventually become his home.

ABOVE *It was the broad and timeless views of the mountainside and sea that attracted Ferri, who even had the electric cables laid underground so that they wouldn't mar the view.*

ABOVE LEFT *One of the five guest houses that make up the Ferri home. These* dammusi *are constructed from unplastered lava stone, with small windows and domed roofs to catch precious drops of rain or even dew.*

LEFT *Ferri's first task was to replace damaged palm trees. New fully grown specimens were imported from Spain and planted around the house, where they provide much needed shade around the outside dining and sitting area.*

RIGHT *The peripatetic photographer imported furniture and fabrics from his many trips abroad to furnish the terraces around his house. These lend a certain exoticism to this holiday home, in tune with the island's multicultural history and its geographical proximity to the shores of northern Africa.*

Based for most of the year in Milan where he works, Ferri had been looking for a place to get away from it all. The *dammusi* that caught his eye and imagination lay derelict in the fertile Valle di Monastero, which makes up the empty southern corner of the island. Christened after a Benedictine monastery that once existed on the site, the solitude and mystical beauty of this landscape that encompassed mountain, sea and a wide arc of sky seemed to present itself as the perfect haven.

After locating the original foundations of the buildings from aerial and infrared photographs, he called in the services of adoptive islander architect Gabriella Giuntoli. Restoring the original structure of *dammusi* took three years; the dimensions had to be precise, twelve-foot square or the entire edifice would crumble in on itself. An impermeable mix of tufa, pumice and chalk paste was smoothed onto the surface of the domed roofs. Telltale cracks on the rooftops were painted with

RIGHT *A planter's chair from India and a length of silk furnish the deck of the outdoor "living room".*

LEFT *By night the dining table glows with candles contained in a collection of Moroccan metal lanterns suspended from the branches. These protect the naked flames from the infamous winds that blow in straight from the Sahara. Most of the produce is grown on the fertile volcanic soil of the property.*

ABOVE *The communal areas of the house spread across different levels on terraces of beaten and polished pumice stone and, sheltered by the shade of clusters of date palms, provide a subtle transition from the dark subdued interiors to the broad open expanses that surround the house.*

LEFT *Oriental copper coffee pots are not only practical – they make a decorative feature of a small niche carved out of the plaster.*

147

ABOVE, LEFT AND RIGHT *The swimming pool has been shaped into the natural landscape. It slopes gently and unobtrusively from a baked earth surround, and its shape has been modelled on Pantelleria's famous volcanic lake, Venus's Mirror. An African canoe sawn in half serves as a dramatic, sculptural throne-like chair.*

a liquid clay in an attractive geometry of lines and crosses, which also perform a practical purpose. Inside the *dammusi*, Giuntoli was puritanical about not using cement or nails to ensure the authenticity and integrity of the traditional form. Walls three-feet thick provide insulation in the winter and a respite from the heat in summer. Likewise, the traditional barrel-vaulted ceilings draw off the heat. The only concession to modernity, apart from electricity and central plumbing, was the installation of glass in the doorway to let in the light and keep out the raging wind.

When it came to the decoration, Ferri created interiors that harmonize with the pervading mood of monastic tranquillity. Furniture is reduced to the bare essentials: a bed, a chest, a basic lamp fashioned from a wrought-iron base with a scroll of parchment paper for a shade, a wooden bowl for shoes, a simple length of suspended bamboo for a clothes rail. Even the showerheads are integrated organically, with water gushing from a stone spout set into the plaster. No pictures, books or curtains clutter up the purity of the space, although a collection of shells or dried flowers might provide modest ornamentation within a stone niche. But while the decor is simple, the effect is never spartan; on the contrary, eclectic and luxurious exoticism is more the hallmark of Ferri's style. Furniture and fabrics collected by the peripatetic photographer on shoots in Africa, India, Bali and Brazil bring a sense of otherworldly glamour to the interiors.

The six bedrooms with individual bathrooms are linked by terraced gardens on different levels planted with myrtle, heather, jasmine and cactus. Shiploads of palm trees were imported from Spain. Banks of prickly pear serve as windbreaks, and the outlying one hundred acres of land have been cultivated for grapes, olive and capers. To counteract the violent climate, the vines are trained low and close to the ground; they produce wines of sweet intensity such as

muscatel. There is a traditional circular Arab garden for the citrus and a vegetable plot providing all the fresh produce needed for the table.

Within this self-sufficient sanctuary, Ferri accentuated the illusion that the modern world has been left far behind by insisting that electricity cables were buried below the ground. "I wanted it to feel like a place outside the normal constraints of time and space.'" No pylons mar the views over mountain and sea, the driveway to the house has been left unasphalted and the swimming pool landscaped so that it looks as though it were part of the natural environment. It slopes gently from a baked-earth surround, its amoebic shape reflecting *Lo Specchio di Venere* – Venus's mirror, the volcanic lake at the centre of the island.

The communal areas are all out-of-doors; dinner and lunch is a movable feast to be enjoyed at one of several tables sheltering in the shade of a palm tree. "Sitting rooms" of hammocks, Balinese beds and floor cushions can be made up or dismantled on a whim. At night, Ferri and his guests sometimes sit out in the fields beneath the expansive sky, in the circle of an old threshing floor. Mattresses, cushions and Moroccan lanterns are arranged around the centrepiece of a shining lump of obsidian retrieved by Ferri from the seabed. Only the sound of the wind rustling the palm leaves and bamboo disturbs the sense of solitude and silence which at Il Monastero is a palpable thing. "It is the sort of pure, primordial experience of the place that is so magical," suggests Ferri, who loves to visit with his wife, the ballerina Alessandra Ferri, even in the winter months when the island is deserted. And if celebrities and urban sophisticates like Sting and Madonna flock here, it is not so much to imbibe a lotus-eating lifestyle as to enjoy a slice of the simple, more spiritual life. With its infamous winds, its volcanic earth, glinting with deposits of obsidian and quartz, the fire that still bubbles beneath the surface and escapes in the form of red-hot springs and geysers, Pantelleria has a dramatic elemental quality quite unlike anywhere else in Italy.

ABOVE *A sculpture and ancient urns decorate a corner of the bathroom.*

ABOVE LEFT AND TOP RIGHT *In the bathrooms, water gushes from a stone spout set in the plaster into a basin carved from soft volcanic rock.*

LEFT *Spare yet exotic furnishings include a simple wrought-iron lamp designed by Ferri and a Thai chest to compliment the antique four-poster Indian bed. The* stucco lustro *effect of the walls and floor – layers of diluted pigment, plaster and lime polished with beeswax – strikes a simple but sophisticated note.*

152

URBAN ELEGANCE

CITY APARTMENTS AND TOWN HOUSES

WHETHER CONCEALED BEHIND the formal façade of a period apartment block in Milan, sheltering in a quiet backwater of Venice or tucked away beneath the eaves above one of Rome's main bustling pedestrian arteries, these secret city retreats are a source of inspiration and surprise. They share an aesthetic based on an element of fantasy and escape, providing a respite, both visual and spiritual, from the pressures and uniform realities of urban life. At their innovative best, these are interiors that marry form and function, design and practicality, and exhibit an extraordinary talent for transforming the mundane and everyday into the beautiful. Exploiting a wide range of decorative materials – wood, wool, silk, leather, glass, resins and plastics – it is the juxtaposition of styles and the mix of classicism, tradition and experimental modernity that defines the interiors of these exotic, eclectic homes.

FIERA DE MILANO APARTMENT

MILAN

ROMEO GIGLI

ABOVE *Romeo Gigli photographed in front of African bark-wood boards.*

ABOVE RIGHT *Mementoes of a globetrotter, with one of Gigli's collection of globes, a symbol of the fashion designer's wanderlust.*

LEFT *An eclectic mix of objects, furniture and ethnic sculptures defines this loft-like space on the top of a 1930s mansion block. A cluster of poufs from Morocco provides a vibrant focal point. The balloon sculptures are by the Iranian Darysh Shokof, the 1950s wooden bench is Japanese by Beorge Nakashima and the circular chair is by Otto Wagner.*

THE WORLD-RENOWNED FASHION DESIGNER Romeo Gigli lives, by necessity, in Milan. By inclination he would rather be as free as a nomad, on the road, in pursuit of the sun and colour of more exotic climes. It is the dream of travel and foreign places, an idea of freedom, that defines the cosmopolitan atmosphere of the city apartment that he shares with his wife Lara and small daughter.

The apartment is located at the top of a 1930s block, in a quiet, residential district of Milan edged with parkland and leafy avenues and squares. It is as close to a green oasis, suggests Gigli, as you are going to get in the heart of the industrial and commercial capital of Italy, where light and space are at a premium. The vast, luminous loft that is his apartment boasts both these precious commodities in abundance. Light floods into the main room from a succession of windows overlooking a garden. It refracts off white glossed walls and polished herringbone parquet to highlight the extraordinarily eclectic mix of objects and furniture. Here, a plethora of tribal handicrafts, naive and ethnic sculptures, contemporary European artwork and furniture classics of the 1950s and 60s coexist in playful harmony. It is a home that truly reflects the free-spirited exuberance and artistic curiosity of its owner – a dynamic space that continually surprises and challenges the eye through the bold and unexpected juxtaposition of colours and diverse shapes and forms.

Gigli delights in the audacious, hence the octopus-like sculptured chandelier, fashioned out of telephone flex by Jacopo Foggini in the dining room, and the Aldo Mondino collages incorporating plastic lighters and carpet samples. He relishes both the sophisticated inventiveness of the installation of musical instruments suspended like a mobile from the living room ceiling, and the naive but equally imaginative collection of ship wall sculptures in his bedroom, made out of driftwood, by a Greek artist from Santorini.

This brand of experimentation also informs his own creations, which embrace many disciplines aside from fashion. The somewhat baroque mirror in the alcove is his own work, as are the sleek aluminium table lamps. Vibrant kilims designed by him lie scattered on the parquet. An exotic mosaic dining room table, also by Gigli, carries a display of glassware, including his own signature vases and jugs, which look as extraordinarily sensuous and soft as fabric draped across a curvaceous limb.

Gigli fell into fashion quite by chance in the late 1970s after a decade of globetrotting, and claims that having had no formal training as a couturier meant he was not restricted by any preconceived notions of style or form. Instead, he drew inspiration from a rich cultural upbringing – from the twenty thousand rare antiquarian books in his bibliophile father's library and from the memory bank of his many travels to the East. In his first collection in the 1980s, and going against the popular trend of power-dressing, he famously wrapped his

ABOVE *Contemporary design and tribal handicrafts coexist in playful harmony. Here, African pygmy drawings on bark-wood boards from West Africa hang behind an American yet Japanese-inspired 1950s floor lamp.*

RIGHT *The cactus sculpture by Guido Drocco and Franco Mello stands next to a red-and-white striped armchair by Antti Nurmesneimi.*

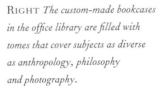

LEFT *Audacious design is the hallmark of the Gigli style. A 1950s chaise longue by Franco Albini sits in front of a collage by Aldo Mondino, featuring carpet samples and cheap throwaway lighters. The mural by Chris Brus extends around the corner of the room to resemble the exterior of an African hut, symbolically marking the threshold of new territory – the separation of the communal open-plan area of the home and the private quarters.*

RIGHT *The custom-made bookcases in the office library are filled with tomes that cover subjects as diverse as anthropology, philosophy and photography.*

Botticelli-like models in soft saris of Thai silk but counterbalanced the oriental femininity of the look with jackets, wool stockings and flat shoes. The decorative spirit in his home is similarly adventurous, exploiting a hybrid of cultural influences.

Amid objects from Burma, India and Japan, the flavour of North Africa appears to predominate with a cluster of brightly coloured leather poufs from Morocco inhabiting the central space of the loft. In one corner, a wall washed in two tones of terracotta, like the exterior of an African hut, symbolically marks the threshold of new territory – the separation between the communal open-plan area of the home, and Gigli and his wife's private quarters. These include a small bedroom taken over by a wardrobe of immaculately colour-coded shirts and trousers, and an opulent bathroom dominated by an exotic mosaic sunken bath.

Gigli creates most of his designs in a studio on a lower floor of the apartment block, which he describes as being as bare and white as a blank sheet of paper, in stark contrast to the explosive colour of the domestic space. His study, separated from the main loft area with

RIGHT *The wall sculptures, made out of flotsam and jetsam found on a beach, are by an artist from the Greek island of Santorini.*

BELOW *The inner sanctum is made up of a colour-coded wardrobe in a corridor, which then leads into the bedroom.*

sliding canvas screens, is where he might come for inspiration. Here, amid the clean abstract modernism of the furniture and furnishings, he surrounds himself with decorative objects that have sentimental appeal: his vast desk is studded with personal, tactile mementoes of journeys, people and places; a pebble sculpted by the sea in Greece, beaded paperweights from New Guinea and shells from the beach. The custom-made bookcases, heaving with tomes that cover subjects as diverse as anthropology, philosophy and photography, reveal the extent of the designer's intellectual curiosity and extensive span of creative reference. Not one, not two, but three globes of the world in different sizes are on display as symbolic totems of Gigli's abiding passion for travel.

And on the balcony, just off the study, he has created an exotic den where he likes to relax and do his thinking. Draped with palm fronds and strewn with cushions, this is another romantic corner of North Africa within the sophisticated confines of the urban sanctum — a secret sanctuary that perhaps helps to appease the insistent wanderlust of Gigli, the globe-trotting couturier.

RIGHT *The dressing room is screened off from the sleeping area with custom-made bookshelves. The wardrobes are immaculately colour-coded, which betrays the disciplined mind working behind Gigli's exuberant creative spirit. The chair beneath the Man Ray painting is by Otto Wagner, one of Gigli's favourite designers.*

160

CASTELLO DISTRICT APARTMENT

MILAN

DONATELLA PELLINI

LEFT *An ornate conservatory looks onto a secret enclosed garden of palm trees and camellia and magnolia blooms. The ornate wrought-ironwork of the balcony and conservatory has been meticulously restored by Donatella and her husband. The glass table was designed by Carlo Mollino in the 1950s.*

ABOVE AND BELOW *The exotic garden, with Donatella Pellini and her dog (below).*

RAFFIC SWIRLS AROUND THE CASTELLO Sforzesco and its adjoining parkland in Milan, but the streets that immediately radiate from the city's major landmark are quiet and exude a sense of solid, northern prosperity. Here, behind the anonymous frontage of a traditional Milanese mansion block, is the luminous, sophisticated apartment of jewellery designer Donatella Pellini and her husband, Vittorio Solbiati, who runs a successful textile business specializing in fine linen.

To step into the *eau-de-nil* hallway, with its turn-of-the-century frescoed cornice panels, stained-glass doorways and stucco flourishes on the ceiling intact, is to breathe the rarefied atmosphere of another era. *The Entertainer* plays on the CD. An aqueous, otherworldly light filters in through the bevelled windows of the art nouveau conservatory, its elaborate wrought-iron framework, so typical of the period, now meticulously restored. This is a quiet space for inspiration. The conservatory looks onto an enclosed garden of palm trees and drooping camellia and magnolia blooms – a secret garden that evokes all the languid sensuality of the *belle époque*. "It doesn't feel like Milan at all," agrees Donatella. "The slightly faded grandeur and romantic exoticism of the garden is much more suggestive of old Sicily."

The interiors, painted in classic shades of the period – old-fashioned lilac, chartreuse, viridian for the study, rose for Donatella's bedroom and aquamarine for a bathroom – also contribute to the sense of nostalgia that permeates the space. "But it is not so much about stylistic correctness," Donatella explains. "The colours were chosen not simply to harmonize with the decorative architecture of the time, but because we find these shades peaceful and relaxing. I love colour both in my jewellery design and in the home."

As slender and effortlessly elegant in her dress as a model from the Charleston era she so admires, Donatella designs a range of accessories from buttons and bags to gloves, hats and, of

163

LEFT *The interiors bring together the best of decorative and furniture design from each decade of the century. A bold 1950s chair by Ico Parisi sits in front of an art deco still life by Orlando Greenwood. The image seems to be repeated in the real display below, featuring a lamp by Fontana Arte and a 1950s vase.*

course, jewellery where she likes to experiment with different metals, glass, resins, crystal and semi-precious stones. Similarly, the apartment embodies her very Italian passion for colour and different textures and mixed media. Fine linens and vintage velvets sit comfortably with the shocking acrylic red of a set of chairs from the 1960s, bought, explains Donatella, "to inject a bit of energy into the dining area". Leather, glass, cane and plastic all have their place in this apartment, which seamlessly fuses decorative elements of the past and present. The gift, it would seem, is in understanding and respecting the spirit of each object.

The couple are flea-market and auction-house addicts, but while Vittorio is a collector of paintings, Donatella's weaknesses are glass and crystal vases and lamps, objects that, beyond their practical function, harness and reflect light. An industrial 1950s metal spotlight, a ceramic and cord lamp from the 1960s, a coloured glass and iron light fixture that is pure art nouveau

RIGHT *The art nouveau decoration in the entrance hall, with its murals, stucco and stained glass, is an original feature of the apartment, dating back to the beginning of the twentieth century, with a flamboyant centrepiece in the shape of a velvet pouf from the Napoleonic period.*

LEFT AND RIGHT *The library,*
which doubles as a dining room, is an
elegy to the feminine grace of the
Liberty style, painted in the strong
viridian green so popular of the
period. The space is dominated by an
enormous nineteenth-century mirror
and an English table from the same
period. The romantic mood is created
by the soft pools of light shed by the
lamps positioned on every surface.
The faux marble fireplace and
stained glass windows are all
original features.

ABOVE *Arrangements of fresh*
flowers fill the interiors with colour
and scent.

or a white sculptural lamp by Kundalini, these lamps from different periods coexist harmoniously. Natural daylight filters through muslin drapes designed by Solbiati, but the romantic mood of the interiors is created by the glow of soft pools of light shed by the variety of lamps positioned on every surface. There are no aggressive hard edges in this house, which appears to be the couple's very private cocoon from the outside world. Even television sets have been banished from the interiors – Donatella and her husband prefer to invite friends round to watch screenings of favourite black-and-white films in the comfort of their private movie theatre.

While in many respects the interiors are an elegy to the grace and romanticism of the *fin-de-siècle* style, this house is by no means a time warp and the decorative spirit is never precious. These interiors bring together the best of decorating and furniture design from each decade of

167

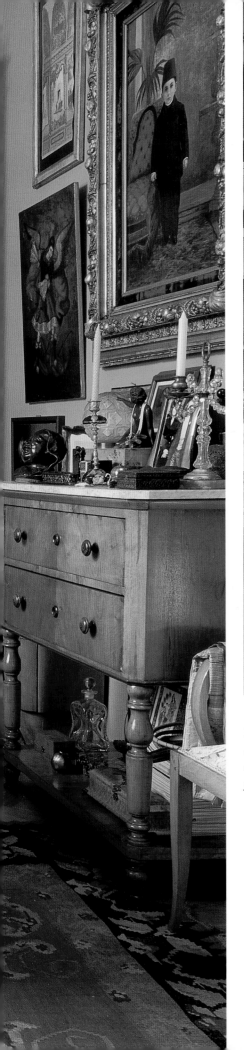

LEFT *The curved bookcase behind Donatella's bed is typical of the so-called* arte povera, *the country furniture made in Lombardy.*

ABOVE *In Donatella's rose-coloured bedroom the style shifts to nostalgic Victorian, with an oriental painting of a Turkish prince in an ornate gold frame lending grandeur to the room.*

RIGHT *Vittorio Solbiati's room is furnished in classic striped wallpaper. The clock in the Empire style is late eighteenth century.*

ABOVE *A mixture of 1930s paintings
and modern furniture characterize this
room. The marble dining table and
Mourn glass are from the 1960s. The
canvas above the mantelpiece is by the
cubist, A Halicka.*

RIGHT *A display of Donatella
jewellery designs in her showroom.*

the century. Nostalgia avoids tipping into sentimentality because the style is kept in check by the injection of the clean abstraction of designs by Fontana Arte, for example, or the high priest of Italian style, Gio Ponti. Their designs vary the pace but without unbalancing the pervading sense of tranquillity. The fluid organic forms of the contemporary furniture and the sinuous, curvilinear shapes of the tables and sofas only help to accentuate the peculiarly sensual and feminine spirit of this house. The apartment, in fact, provides a continual oasis of colour and light as a balanced antithesis to where it is situated; in the hard-edged commercial city that is Milan.

CASTELLO DISTRICT TOWN HOUSE
VENICE

ALISTAIR AND ROMILLY McALPINE

LEFT *A garden is a luxury in Venice where land is at a premium. David Wynne's slender towering bronzes of Mary Magdalene and Christ seem to merge with self-seeded figs and other shrubs, which grow skyward in this enclosed space.*

RIGHT *The McAlpines' house is located in the quiet district of Castello, next to the crenellated walls of the Arsenale, a vast dockyard and monument to the Republic's one-time maritime supremacy.*

BELOW *Romilly McAlpine and Petrushka aboard their private motor launch, upholstered in cotton for the summer and McAlpine tartan in winter.*

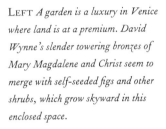

S TEPS AWAY FROM THE GUIDECCA, THE Grand Canal and St Mark's Square – the sumptuous and much-photographed façades of Venice – is the tranquil district, or *sestiere*, of Castello. Hidden within the eastern sector, this is the domestic face of the city. It is a "peopled labyrinth of walls" in Shelley's words, where the streets belong not to marauding tourists but to those who live here – gossiping matrons and quiet artisans and a colony of cats. The only grandiose landmark of the area is the Arsenale, the finest monument to the Republic's one-time maritime supremacy. For centuries, the dockyard with its impressive triumphal arch and crenellated towers, saw the repairs and construction of a navy that was the basis of Venice's might and wealth. Today, lines of drying laundry rather than emblazoned banners tend to festoon the tranquil alleyways.

For the last decade, the Castello has also been home to Lord and Lady McAlpine. Their house, at the edge of a quiet *campo* next to a lazy canal, lies concealed behind a suitably anonymous façade. The nineteenth-century building, which once housed three separate families and a paper press, was not chosen for its rare architectural merits. However, because it was not a fine palazzo, it meant the McAlpines could gain possession of the property without being tangled up in bureaucratic red tape. "Otherwise you wouldn't be able to drive a single nail into the plaster or make major structural alterations as we did, without having to wait years for sheaths of authorizations," explains Lady McAlpine.

When the former Treasurer and Deputy Chairman of the Conservative Party had his English country estate blown up by terrorists, Venice was the one city he and his wife Romilly could both agree on as an alternative home. With a low crime rate, no cars and no pollution, it represented a secure and tranquil haven for themselves and their young daughter. "You can wander the streets alone at night and still feel safe," says Romilly. "It combines all the best

LEFT *The surprising juxtaposition of different objects and styles gives the entrance hall a theatrical quality. Here, Venetian light sconces frame a fireplace and an ornate custom-made cabinet houses rare latte cina glass that looks as milky white as porcelain. A life-size papier mâché figure of San Gerolamo by Joe Tilson adds a surreal note.*

RIGHT *The library is a showcase for some of Lord McAlpine's collections. Here the vibrant colours of local Murano glassware, displayed on top of the bookshelves, are repeated in the deep jewel tones of the furnishings and sofas by Carlo Mollino. A bronze sculpture of a pope by Manzu stands on top of the plinth.*

LEFT *Contemporary furniture makes a bold statement on a corner of the staircase, with a dramatic red light fitting by Carlo Moretti set above a chair by Enri de Breuil.*

LEFT *The entrance hall, which doubles as a dining room, gets little natural light, but rough beamed ceilings and the terrazzo floor bring warmth to the interior. The capitals on the walls are by British architect Quinlan Terry – a temporary display taking the place of a collection of Vivienne Westwood shoes that are on loan for an exhibition.*

RIGHT *Above the fireplace, two Roman busts beneath a resin mirror add grandeur and stature to the room.*

aspects of the countryside and town." It is provincial in the best sense of the word; here, in the shops, bars and markets, everyone knows you by name and life unfolds at a slower pace – a much welcomed respite from all the frenetic activity of the Thatcher years of government. Yet Venice, Napoleon's "drawing room of Europe", remains the most cosmopolitan, civilized of cities, its reputation founded on a cultural and social openness that continues to attract curious travellers, very much like the McAlpines, from around the world.

The McAlpines' house, however, is less a drawing room or stage set for formal entertaining and more a place of refuge. It is also something of a rich storehouse for Alistair's and Romilly's prodigious collections: his libraries, objets d'art and contemporary paintings; her extraordinary wardrobe, which is stored in a separate studio at the side of the garden and catalogued by number onto the computer. While the peaceful enclosed garden, the terrace and hallway are sometimes used for dinner parties (more formal dinners are now often hosted at the Hotel Monaco or Cipriani instead), the official dining room has been completely overtaken by beads. Rare and precious excavation finds from Tibet, Yemen, Ethiopia, Venice and Indonesia are graded by region and design into neat boxes. Others spill kaleidoscopically from trays like gobstoppers in an old-fashioned sweet shop.

Alistair's passion for colour extends not only to the beads but also finds expression in the vivid contemporary objets d'art that catch the eye at every turn. Luminous local glassware from Murano is displayed in cabinets in the living room and on top of the bookcases in the library. In the hallway he has light-heartedly juxtaposed colourful Vivienne Westwood shoes on pedestals next to classical bronzes and a lifesize papier-mâché figure of San Gerolamo by Joe Tilson, an Italy-based abstract artist much admired by Alistair. In this house, the quirky arrangement of the objects and furnishing seems to make a statement that

LEFT AND RIGHT *Steel, glass resin, wood and stone are all represented in the collection of contemporary objets d'art, displayed against a neutral yet elegant backdrop of pale parquet and white walls. On the mantelpiece, plaster figurines by Sidney Nolan stand either side of an enigmatic Roman head. Glassware from Romeo Gigli is displayed between the sconces and on tables, both by Mark Brazier Jones. The primitive forms of the sculptures by Bill Turnbull in the foreground contrast dramatically with the intricate frivolity of the chandelier by Debbie Thomas.*

BELOW LEFT *The abstract, vibrant canvas, hung above the plain white sofa, is another work by Joe Tilson.*

is as much intellectual as decorative. After all, why shouldn't a well-made shoe not be given the same prominence and authority as the antique bust of a Roman emperor or a paper-and-glue saint?

Romilly's tastes veer more to the minimalist. She influenced the choice of white walls and plain wooden parquet or marble as a neutral backdrop that would not fight with such a vibrant profusion of things. The monochrome simplicity of the bedroom makes it her favourite room of the house. It synthesizes the clean lines of 1940s and 50s art deco furniture with the melting curves of Gio Ponti's chairs and Giacometti's wall sculpture of a dove. "Venice is a city of exuberant beautiful colour: you could overdose on all it. When I close the doors on the world, I hanker for the soothing restraint of white: white walls, white linen, the lingering balm of white flowers, Casablanca lilies especially."

The garden is another sanctuary and a luxurious feature for Venice, where land is at such a premium. Completely enclosed and sheltered from the sun, the plants grow skyward, tall and

straight. Slim and enigmatic sculptures by David Wynne follow the towering lines of the vegetation and seem to inhabit the space. "Inside each piece there is a spirit trying to break out. His works are not just dead lumps of bronze of marble," enthuses Alistair in his memoirs, *Once a Jolly Bagman*. The same sense of fluidity and energy may be said to characterize the spirit of this house. Despite the rarity of the collections and the fine aesthetic sensibilities of the proprietors, this is a most un-museum-like home. The displays are never static. Collections grow and migrate constantly, mutating according to the changing spaces which define them. An object like a shoe can have a practical purpose, but suspended on a plinth it takes on an artistic presence of its own. The broad amalgam of styles contained in objects and collections that embrace both antiquity and modernity, the practical and the purely decorative, informs the unique and exhilarating atmosphere of this house.

ABOVE AND RIGHT *The monochromatic bedroom exudes tranquillity, synthesizing the clean restrained lines of 1940s and 50s furniture with the soft curves of Carlo Mollino chairs and a Giacommetti wall sculpture of an albatross. The four-poster bed in aluminium is a first design by Tony Little from the 1960s; lamps and the chest of drawers are by the Italian modernist Gio Ponti, while the table is also by Carlo Mollino.*

SPANISH STEPS APARTMENT
ROME

GIANCARLO GIAMMETTI

ABOVE AND ABOVE RIGHT
The terraces overlooking the rooftops of Rome are what seduced Giancarlo Giammetti into buying this top-floor apartment, a former dance studio. These more than compensate for the restraints of space within.

LEFT *The subdued tones of these sumptuous interiors provide a soothing counterpoint to the colour and chaos of the streets outside. There is drama and energy, too, provided most strikingly by the owner's extraordinary art collection. Here, a vast oil by Balthus,* Le Chat au Miroir, *provides a provocative edge.*

GIANCARLO GIAMMETTI, THE FORMER chief executive and business brain behind the Valentino fashion empire, lives, quite appropriately, on Rome's most famous shopping street off the Spanish Steps. This is also the heart of baroque Rome, once colonized by wide-eyed foreigners on the Grand Tour. Many of them, including Tennyson and Thackeray, resided at the old English Club in the Palazzo Lepri.

Today the top floors of this eighteenth-century palazzo, once servants' quarters, have been transformed into a bijou residence to suit the exacting tastes of the urbane Signor Giammetti. With the help of architect Peter Marino, he has transformed the once dingy, low-ceilinged rooms into the ultimate sophisticated pied-à-terre. He was seduced, above all, by the terraces which more than compensated for the restraints of space. "If you're lucky enough to enjoy a view such as this, you are not necessarily going to get a flat with lofty ceilings like the Sistine Chapel." And coming from the quiet leafy Roman suburbs of Parioli, he was thirsty for a neighbourhood that breathed theatre.

From here, Giammetti could walk to work through the Piranesi-esque bustle of Piazza di Spagna, a short stroll away. Here too, from the vantage point of his terrace, was a panorama that gave him Rome in all its cinematic splendour. In the distance the cupolas of Bramante jostle for space against Romanesque spires. Closer up, it is a *tableau vivant* of jumbled terracotta roof tiles along which a cat walks the tightrope between windowsill and gutter, while in the pensione opposite a visitor to Rome may hang his washing out to dry over the unsuspecting heads of the serial shoppers below. And, stage right, there is the majestic sweep of the Spanish Steps themselves, where colourful cascades of azalea compete for space next to guitar-strumming students and camera-wielding tourists.

LEFT AND ABOVE *The walnut desk is eighteenth-century French (left), with secret compartments, and sits well with other equally extravagant pieces of furniture, such as the nineteenth-century Chinese lacquered box with mother-of-pearl inlay (above).*

RIGHT *Bevelled mahogany bookcases with concealed lighting in the leather-covered front panels throw a warm glow on a collection of old and rare books bought from a Tuscan estate. The opulent effect comes not only from the furniture and objets d'art but also from the fine textures used in the furnishings: custom-made Thai silk for the walls, flat woven wool for the carpets, mushroom-coloured taffeta and linen for the curtains, and velvet and leather for sofas and chair. An audacious François Lalanne crocodile chair in bronze from the 1970s is placed thus, so that it ruffles the prevailing mood of ordered serenity.*

But the colour, cacophony and convivial chaos of the streets are left behind on entering Giammetti's monochromatic apartment. Stepping into the chiaroscuro of the entrance hall and main salon, the shafts of bright sunlight that penetrate the hushed interior through heavy drapes serve only to accentuate the depth of the shadows. This is a perfectionist's retreat built around a disciplined decorative scheme of black on white, interspersed with shades of ivory and charcoal. A custom-made chocolate-brown silk from Thailand lines the walls, while polished mahogany bookcases and parquet flooring stained black provide a sober backdrop for Giammetti's extraordinary collection of objets d'art, acquired mostly through dealers and in auctions abroad. Cunningly concealed uplighters and downlighters dramatically illuminate the library of beautifully bound books and an eclectic mix of objects with an Eastern accent: lacquer and tortoiseshell boxes, Chinese ivory and porcelain. To

ABOVE LEFT *Robert Mapplethorpe's graphic black-and-white photographs of flowers frame a collection of tribal masks.*

ABOVE RIGHT *Picasso's* Buste de Femme *(1954) sits above a German sculpture of a horse skeleton and between a pair of eighteenth-century iron urns.*

RIGHT *What was once a rooftop service pavilion is now the master bedroom. The strict precision of the interior design is softened by the use of tactile furnishings and walls luxuriously upholstered by architect Peter Marino in panels of horsehair. An Empire bed sits between Josef Hoffman cabinets, set either side of a painting by Tony Sherman.*

remove one ornament would be to upset the harmony and balance of the space and the oriental mood of ordered serenity. This is Giammetti's "ivory tower", his sanctuary from the outside world where, above all, he likes to be alone. It is also, however, a sufficiently versatile space to enable him to host large groups of people, and when he does entertain, it is on a lavish scale.

The L-shaped space of the lower floor is carved up into separate areas for reading, writing, conversation and dining. To create the illusion of space and height, Marino worked on the principle of the clean unbroken line. The only curves appear in the odd sloping shoulder of a vase or the elegant droop of a porcelain heron's neck. However, the strict masculine precision of the interior is softened by the use of tactile textured fabrics and furnishings: a flat woven carpet in the blondest wool, dark and golden velvets for the upholstery, tobacco-coloured taffeta for the curtains, old leather for an armchair, horsehair panels for the bedrooms upstairs. "I belong to the touchy-feely school of design," explains Marino, "and this is all haute-couture." Given the erstwhile profession of the proprietor, this all makes perfect sense.

The real drama of the apartment, however, comes from the paintings. The artwork Giammetti collects is bold and audacious. There is an Andy Warhol, a Modigliani, a few sketches by Henri Matisse and a Pablo Picasso over the fireplace. In the bedroom hang Robert Mapplethorpe's intriguing black-and-white photographs of flowers that are reproduced in the flesh with minimalist arrangements of sculptural arum lilies or tulips in vases.

ABOVE AND RIGHT *The geometry of an inlaid mahogany floor and the strategically positioned Francis Bacon,* Figure Turning, *add depth and perspective to a small hallway. The Empire style is represented in the chairs and the columns, most of them dating from the end of the nineteenth century, while Zoran's* Music *oil on canvas (1989) is displayed behind a bronze statue of a horse.*

LEFT *The dining room is decorated with Italian chinoiserie panels in leather, and parchment cabinets designed by architect Peter Marino. To create the illusion of space and height, Marino worked on the principle of the clean unbroken line. The only curves appear in the odd sloping shoulder of a Chinese vase or the arch of a porcelain heron's neck.*

Downstairs in the hallway, the perspective of Francis Bacon's mysterious *Figure Turning* beckons you in. A vast Balthus canvas dominates the living room. Its enigmatic composition, suggesting both innocence and knowledge, is provocative and unsettling. As Giammetti explains, "You have to have a little lemon juice to make a room interesting." And so in amongst the elegant sophistication of Empire, French art deco and eighteenth-century furniture, there is a contemporary François Lalanne chair in bronze, with a crocodile curved along the back rest. "It provides shock value; friends either love it or loathe it." And then, casting an appraising glance across his domain, he adds "But isn't it always like this when you have something unique?"

189

VISITORS' GUIDE

THE TORRE DI BELLOSGUARDO
This hotel can be visited all year round.
2 Via Roti Michelozzi
Florence 50124
Tel: +39 (055) 22 98 145
Fax: +39 (055) 02 29 008

CASTELLO ROMITORIO
To buy wines from Chia's estate, contact:
Tel: +39 (057) 78 97 220
Fax: +39 (057) 78 97 026
by email:
info@castelloromitorio.it
On the estate there are an old water mill and farmhouse available for rent. Contact:
Tel: +39 (057) 78 97 220
Fax: +39 (057) 78 97 026
by email: cavittor@tim.it

CASTELLO RUSPOLI
To visit the gardens, open from April to October on Sundays from 10am to 1pm, contact:
Tel: +39 (076) 17 55 338

PALAZZO PARISI
For information on how to rent the houses, refer to Lady Lennox-Boyd's office in London:
Tel: +44 (020) 7931 9995
by email:
arabellalennoxboyd.com

PALAZZO BELMONTE
A wing of the seventeenth-century estate overlooking the sea has been converted into an hotel, with five acres of parkland, a swimming pool and private beach.
Tel: +39 (097) 40 60 211
Fax: +39 (097) 49 61 150
www.palazzobelmonte.it

CASTELLO DEPRESSA
Wine Shop at:
Castel del Salve on
via Tempio 24 Tricase
Puglia
Antiques shop at:
P. Castello 8
Depressa
Tel: +39 (083) 37 76 008

CAMILLA GUINNESS'S SHOP
Via Soccini
44 Buonconvento
Siena
Tel: +39 (057) 78 06 389
Fax: +39 (057) 78 06 389

IL MONASTERO
For information about renting the dammusi, contact:
Tel: +39 (02) 58 1861
Fax: +39 (02) 58 1862 89
www.monasteropantelleria.com

LE FONTANELLE
For information on renting houses on the estate and Castellini designs, contact:
Piero Castellini shop
Via della Spiga no. 50
Milan
Tel: +39 (02) 78 0257
Fax: +39 (02) 78 0501

Piero Castellini showroom:
Ferno VA
Via G Flacone no. 12
Tel: +39 (033) 17 26 140

Contact in UK:
Grafton House
2/3 Golden Square
London W1F 9HR
Tel: +44 (020) 7494 72737

DONATELLA PELLINI
Via Manzoni 20
Tel: +39 (02) 76 00 8084

ROMEO GIGLI
via della spiga 30
Tel: +39 (02) 76 01 1983
Fax: +39 (02) 76 01 1919

BIBLIOGRAPHY

BLUE GUIDE: SOUTHERN ITALY by Paul Blanchard (*WW Norton & Company*)

GORE VIDAL by Fred Kaplan (*Bloomsbury*)

INSIGHT GUIDE: NORTHERN ITALY (*Langenscheidt*)

ITALIA – THE ART OF LIVING ITALIAN STYLE by Edmund Howard (*Weidenfeld & Nicolson*)

ITALIAN ART, LIFE AND LANDSCAPE by Bernard Wall (*Heinemann*)

ITALIAN ISLANDS by Dana Facaros and Michael Pauls (*Cadogan Guides*)

ITALIAN STYLE by Jane Gordon Clark (*Frances Lincoln*)

ITALY – A GRAND TOUR FOR THE MODERN TRAVELLER by Charles Fitzroy (*Macmillan*)

THE LAST LEOPARD by David Gilmour (*The Harvill Press*)

THE LEOPARD by Giuseppe Tomasi di Lampedusa (*Pantheon Books*)

LIVING IN VENICE by Frederick Vitoux (*Flammarion*)

NORTHERN LAZIO – AN UNKNOWN ITALY by Wayland Kennett and Elizabeth Young (*John Murray*)

ONCE A JOLLY BAGMAN by Alistair McAlpine (*Weidenfeld & Nicolson*)

ROME AND THE HEART OF ITALY by Dana Facaros and Michael Pauls (*Cadogan Guides*)

SOUTH ITALY by Paul Holberton (*John Murray*)

A TRAVELLER IN SOUTHERN ITALY by HV Morton (*Methuen*)

TUSCANY by Dana Facaros and Michael Pauls (*Cadogan Guides*)

VILLA DETAILS by Ovidio Guaita (*Cartago*)

WITHIN TUSCANY by Matthew Spender (*Viking*)

INDEX

Page numbers in *italics* refer to illustrations.

ACKNOWLEDGMENTS

I would like to thank all the owners of these beautiful houses for their time and unfailing hospitality, especially Camilla and Jasper, Claudia, Romilly, Matthew and Maro, Gaia, Marella, Guki Dickie Francesco, Sandro and Inge Feltrinelli who put me up on various occasions over the years and who made even the shortest stopover seem like a summer holiday. Thanks also to Lucy Clive for an invaluable introduction, to Melissa Whitworth for her support, to Marina Sersale for Positano and to the Sestis for providing shelter and fun in the middle of storms, floods, broken Hasselblads and the *vendemnia*. Mark Luscombe-Whyte was a reliable source of patience and humour. And I am, of course, particularly grateful to my parents who brought me, as a toddler, to live in Italy in the first place. CF